Praise for

WINNING WITH

UNDERDOGS

and Gil Winch

Gil Winch is a pioneer in creating opportunities for people who have been underestimated and overlooked. In this insightful, inspiring book, he shows you how to find diamonds in the rough and help them reach their potential. I can't think of anyone better to teach us how to build a workplace that's both more inclusive and more effective.

—**Adam Grant,** #1 *New York Times* bestselling author of *Think Again* and host of the TED podcast *WorkLife*

In *Winning with Underdogs*, Gil offers a proven path to create workplaces that are truly inclusive to all, achieving a kind of justice we have failed to accomplish elsewhere. He gives us actionable advice on how to overcome bias and create environments that help people feel safe and do their best work. But there is also another point: when we look for potential in people, we often use a strategy that is competitive and aggressive, which yields a particular kind of winner and misses the rich potential that exists not only in underdogs but in all of us. Gil brings to light the structural inequities in our workplaces and helps us understand how we can uncover and cultivate potential in all people.

—**Corey Hajim,** Business Curator at TED Conferences

In this provocative work, Dr. Gil Winch makes a convincing case that our diversity and inclusion initiatives aren't inclusive enough. Through the inspiring story of his own business and many other examples, he shows us the overlooked potential of underdogs and outlines the real accommodations and practical strategies needed to reveal that potential. If you've ever sensed that diversity and inclusion initiatives are often mostly performative, and want to do better, you'll learn how through this moving book.

> —**Alice Boyes,** PhD, author of *The Anxiety Toolkit* and *Stress-Free Productivity* and contributor to *Harvard Business Review*

Winch invites leaders to prioritize the most important asset of any organization: the employees. By adopting a truly inclusive approach, leaders will dramatically transform the organizational culture, improve engagement, and create real happiness in the workplace, while increasing productivity. Using his own company as a use case, he shows how to put theory into practice and drive true and lasting positive change.

> —**Yiftah Yoffe,** VP of Human Resources at Check Point Software Technologies, Ltd.

The underdogs are people with disabilities who were denied decent and respectful employment because of their status. In the company he established, Winch puts aside the dis-, focuses on abilities, and proves that their level of performance is comparable to able-bodied workers. In the process, he uses a most creative, personal, and humanistic managerial approach that should be applied in any workplace and should be studied in business schools! He also makes the case regarding the central role of regular, gainful employment in the process of rehabilitation of people with a variety of physical and mental dysfunctions. Touching on the personal, organizational, and policy levels, this book is a must-read for anyone who manages people in a workplace.

> —**Benjamin Gidron,** Professor Emeritus at the Guilford Glazer Faculty of Management at Ben Gurion University

WINNING WITH
UNDERDOGS

WINNING WITH
UNDERDOGS

How Hiring the Least Likely Candidates
Can Spark Creativity, Improve Service,
and Boost Profits for Your Business

GIL WINCH

NEW YORK   CHICAGO   SAN FRANCISCO   ATHENS   LONDON
MADRID   MEXICO CITY   MILAN   NEW DELHI
SINGAPORE   SYDNEY   TORONTO

1 2 3 4 5 6 7 8 9   LCR   27 26 25 24 23 22

ISBN: 978-1-264-27491-8
MHID   1-264-27491-2

e-ISBN: 978-1-264-27492-5
e-MHID: 1-264-27492-0

Design by Lee Fukui and Mauna Eichner

Library of Congress Cataloging-in-Publication Data

Names: Winch, Gil, author.
Title: Winning with underdogs : why hiring underdogs is good for business
   and how you can leverage it for success / Gil Winch.
Description: New York : McGraw Hill, [2023] | Includes bibliographical
   references and index.
Identifiers: LCCN 2022015385 (print) | LCCN 2022015386 (ebook) | ISBN
   9781264274918 (hardback) | ISBN 9781264274925 (ebook)
Subjects: LCSH: Diversity in the workplace. | Employee selection. |
   Minorities—Employment. | Corporate culture. | Social responsibility of
   business. | Success in business.
Classification: LCC HF5549.5.M5 W558 2023 (print) | LCC HF5549.5.M5
   (ebook) | DDC 658.3008—dc23/eng/20220401
LC record available at https://lccn.loc.gov/2022015385
LC ebook record available at https://lccn.loc.gov/2022015386

McGraw Hill books are available at special quantity discounts to use as premiums and sales promotions or for use in corporate training programs. To contact a representative, please visit the Contact Us pages at www.mhprofessional.com.

McGraw Hill is committed to making our products accessible to all learners. To learn more about the available support and accommodations we offer, please contact us at accessibility@mheducation.com. We also participate in the Access Text Network (www.accesstext.org), and ATN members may submit requests through ATN.

To all CY employees—past, present, and future
To all those left out who wish to be let in
To all those dedicated to letting them in

Contents

PART III

GETTING FROM HERE TO THERE

Acknowledgments

I would like to thank my agent, Michelle Tessler, who coached and encouraged me through five versions of the book proposal until I finally found the correct way to tell this story. She is an incredibly dedicated agent, and I'm so lucky to have her. Huge thanks to my developmental editor, Kevin Commins, and my editor at McGraw Hill, Casey Ebro, whose valuable and insightful edits and comments truly elevated the manuscript. Working with them was a wonderful partnership and a pleasure. I would also like to thank my readers, especially Eran Segev and Guy Shelly for their time and many helpful suggestions.

CY, and by consequence, this book, wouldn't have succeeded without the help and kindness of many people: my fairy godfather Hezy Bador, our hero Liza Hadash, Yuval Arad, Amit Pines, Yuval Wagner, Yoachim Schoss, Yoram Raviv, Tammy Arad, Ilan Raviv, Dan Geva, Zvi Zilbermintz, Shirit Zaks Haim, Idit Moshe, Israel Venture Network (IVN), and Haim Ben Yaakov and his wonderful team of lawyers whose pro bono work has saved dozens of our employees over the years. Lastly, our dear friend Udi Segal, our knight in shining armor whose compassionate support and reporting helped save the day time and again.

I would also like to thank my wonderful board of directors who for years have volunteered their time and wisdom to join in the fight for underdog inclusion in the workplace—Claudio Yarza, Tovit Yair, Jackie Goren, Haim Ariel, and Danny Zur, who has fought on our behalf from day one. We wouldn't be here without his support and kindness.

My deep thanks, love, and admiration to the amazing management team at CY, headed by Pnina, our deputy CEO, the most dedicated, competent, and inspiring leader I could have hoped for; Ayelet, the dynamo of our HR; Amir, my dear friend, our first CEO turned head of rehabilitation, a true Mahatma; Maxim, Margalit, Nofar, and Hava. Our truly extraordinary team leaders who deliver the impossible daily: Gila, Nataly, Yasmin, Ismail, Liz, Dikla, and Sophie. And all CY employees—past, present, and future—you inspire me every day.

Thanks to my twin brother and soulmate, Guy Winch, who cheered me on throughout. His writing and storytelling have thrilled and inspired me since we were five years old. Thanks to my daughters, Ori and Shiri, whose love will forever be my inspiration and motivation.

And lastly, thanks to my wife, Efrati, who has shared every step of this 20-year emotional roller coaster of a journey we've been on. I have never met anyone so capable, so beautiful, and with so much talent, love, and such extraordinary caring for others. This is as much your story as it is mine. Forever my love.

Author's Note

I believe with all my heart that we are indeed all equal, that our diversity is a source of our strength, and that differences in beliefs, color, gender, preferences, and abilities should be celebrated, not used to divide. However, writing about diversity and social justice can be tricky. Many people's nerves are so frayed from years of marginalization and exclusion that even the smallest unintended infraction or incorrect terminology can cause severe pain and angst, which is the last thing I want.

Alas, I am far from perfect, and I'm sure that now or in the future, my attempts at using the correct and proper language might be found wanting, especially considering that the right terminology changes every few years.

This book is a work driven by love, and I would hate for anyone to take offense. Any mistakes in this regard are my own and were made unintentionally and inadvertently. I would ask that in such cases, you judge leniently, balance the scales by taking into account the past 20 years of my endeavors, and chalk up any slipups or insensitivities to a lack of attention rather than a lack of respect.

WINNING WITH UNDERDOGS

Introduction

Most people don't realize how close we actually are to socially transforming our world. At long last we've arrived at this unique time in human history, where technology, a camera in each hand, and social media afford us the opportunity to substantially reduce social injustice around the globe. Traditional and social media drag various social injustices out of the shadows, with our smartphones providing dramatic live footage of daily bias discrimination and prejudice, laying them bare for all to see.

We can no longer pretend that inequality isn't widespread and deep-rooted. Seeing it with our own eyes wakes us up, galvanizes us, and hardens our resolve, pushing many of us to fight for changes in our society. We post, we shout, and we protest in the streets. National and global public sentiment is ripe for a historical collective push toward social justice and real equality. Yet, despite our intentions, I fear that we might not achieve the changes for which we're fighting.

I've been an organizational psychologist for 35 years, and the long duration of my career has offered me diverse experiences. I've worked with a variety of industries, such as finance, retail, manufacturing, and high tech, and with top-security-clearance–required governmental entities. I've worked within all levels of an organization, from entry-level to C-suite employees, and I've served as the personal consultant to Israel's chief of police, industry leaders, and heads of large organizations. I've also given keynotes and workshops to business leaders and executives from over 70 countries.

Among these industries, corporations, cultures, and nations, I've observed a single overarching similarity: marginalized populations are in general underrepresented or disadvantaged in the workforce, and some populations are practically absent from it, regardless of where you are in the world. This global phenomenon of workplace exclusion seems to follow similar rules of thumb across nations. And it's not just marginalized populations and small fringe groups who suffer continued workplace inequality. It's shockingly most of the globe's population when you do the math.

In the United States, Black and Hispanic people represent 32 percent of the population but suffer significantly higher levels of unemployment than white people.[1] Moreover, according to the U.S. Federal Reserve, "the typical White family has eight times the wealth of the typical Black family and five times the wealth of the typical Hispanic family."[2] Perhaps more astonishing, women—half of the global population—are paid less than men *in every country on the planet.*

The global gender parity gap in 2020
was at 31.4 percent.[3]

Founded in 1903 in the United Kingdom by Emmeline Pankhurst, the suffragettes fought for women's right to vote. It took 25 years of protests, hunger strikes, and thousands of incarcerations to win that basic right. But bias and bigotry toward women continues 80 years later, as women have yet to achieve equal opportunities and wages, and they are, still, sexually harassed with shocking frequency (in a recent survey 81 percent of women reported experiencing sexual harassment in their lifetime[4]). Over 50 years ago, a million people marched with Martin Luther King Jr. for racial justice and equality. Yet after all that time and effort, Black people are regularly shot and victimized just because of the color of their skin.

> Minority men's rate of board representation in the Fortune 500 grew at less than 0.5 percent per year from 2010 to 2020. African American/Black men lost one seat in the Fortune 100 and five seats in the Fortune 500.[5]

Despite the growing public outcry, something hasn't fully worked with our prolonged attempts to end social injustice, and it doesn't seem to be lack of motivation or caring. People are active and vocal, and many who were quiet in the past are quiet no more. Women, people of color, and other groups that are fighting for social justice actually constitute a large majority in the United States.

If such a large majority of people deeply desire a change that is not only just and honorable but also greatly beneficial to all and is a change that has few detractors (as we shall see), why are we still fighting for it? Why hasn't it happened already? What is holding back the change? Apparently, we seem to be missing something, overlooking something, neglecting something crucial. Indeed, we are, and I want to explain what I think that something is. It's corporate America, it's businesses. It's our workplaces. Social justice needs to start there.

The workplace is where people from all walks of life meet, strive to move ahead, endeavor to provide for their loved ones, and hope to afford themselves and their families a better life. Those are the natural and widespread motivations and dreams of most individuals in a capitalist society, and employed adults spend most of their waking hours at their workplace pursuing them. For most adults, the workplace represents the focal point of our time, the doorway to our aspirations, and the place we go to provide for our daily needs. The modern-day workplace is a powerful entity indeed.

According to a 2021 survey, 66 percent of employees have experienced workplace bullying.[6]

Yet, our workplaces are currently hotbeds of social injustice and widespread exclusion (some of the data I'll present is indeed staggering). Many large corporations actively conceal their exclusion of various groups and minorities while publishing glowing articles and reports touting the importance of diversity, equity, and inclusion (DE&I) and their own "commitment" to full inclusion and social justice. I'll introduce data proving that in the modern-day workplace, too many marginalized groups are underrepresented and often disadvantaged simply because they belong to a "nonmainstream" group (people of color, people with disabilities, ex-convicts, older people, shy and anxious people, various minorities, and so on) and because of our many biases.

If you believe that you are immune from such disregard, give it time. Given that age is one of the causes of employment marginalization, most of us will join the employment underdog ranks eventually, and, sadly, many of us will not have to wait until later in life to do so. During the span of our work life, countless people will experience periods during which our self-confidence and self-efficacy dip and our anxiety peaks—and for some of us, unemployment will become chronic.

It's so regrettable that the workplace has been largely neglected in our voiced outrage and cries for equality because it is such a crucial venue when attempting to deal with social injustice. Most of us experience and witness exclusion and prejudice at our workplaces, but often we dismiss or disregard such occurrences for various reasons. We are hesitant to "make a fuss" or "tangle" with a superior because such actions could have ominous consequences to our own job. But we also tend to view ourselves as good and honorable people, and we would like to see ourselves acting with integrity in the face of social injustice.

Faced with an incongruence between our (in)actions and our values and self-beliefs, our psyche often resolves such inner conflicts and discrepancies by "interpreting" the offending incident as insignificant, minor, or "someone just having a bad day," thus reducing its potency in our mind's eye and keeping our integrity complete. At times our subconscious will protect us by not even noticing troubling events, by glossing over them altogether. Alas, by subconsciously allowing ourselves to put up with such incidents at one place, we render our efforts to eliminate them elsewhere psychologically weaker and lacking in resolve. Believing, subconsciously or otherwise, that we are powerless to change upsetting injustices in the workplace saps our will and strength to fight them in general, and it allows the exclusion of many of our brothers and sisters to continue.

We should turn our collective gaze toward the workplace not just because of its importance in the greater fight for equality and social justice, and not just because its cruel exclusion of various groups must end. We should turn our collective gaze toward bringing social justice to the workplace because it's so beneficial to us all. Any society that maximizes its resources and production capabilities will have greater combined wealth because when more unemployed people join the workforce and become contributing and productive members of an economy, that economy grows and becomes richer.

If all noninstitutionalized adults in the United States had a job (a stat called *U-6*, which is the most accurate stat regarding the growth potential of a workforce), the US national workforce would grow by 10 percent on average. That's an additional 15 to 16 million jobs added, which would turboboost the national economy, significantly improving the conditions and wealth of every household in the country. It goes without saying that it would greatly affect the lives of those 15 to 16 million new employees and their families, transforming them from the unwanted status of dependents to proud contributing assets.

Full inclusion can create financial benefits that are no less than dramatic not only for the nation as a whole but also for corporate America and large companies alike, which we will detail in Chapter 1. For both our communities and for businesses, the benefits of full inclusion are similarly profound. Last but not least, for our employment-deprived brothers and sisters—the employment underdogs themselves—as we shall see, the difference between chronic unemployment and a steady job is literally life changing and at times even lifesaving.

Because of its profound importance to us and because of the huge potential gains to all, the workplace must become the key arena to achieve real social justice, true acceptance, and equality:

> We deserve to go to work among people who differ from ourselves, people who represent the real diversity of our communities.

> We deserve to exchange the fears that such differences currently evoke with comfort in the understanding that those members of our community who are different from ourselves strengthen us, complete us, and even proudly define us as a community.

> We deserve to feel that powerful bond between brothers in arms who share the same workplace and the same purpose, striving for the collective good of our families while strengthening the community we share.

> We deserve to know that we can happily invest our best efforts without fearing that our accomplishments and individual worth will be overshadowed by our gender, color, or beliefs and that we can be confident that we are judged on our merits alone, free of any bias.

We deserve to feel safe, supported, and cared for at the place we spend most of our waking hours, without fear of harassment, bullying, or mistreatment.

We deserve to work in workplaces that cater to our emotional needs as much as our physical needs, organizations that respect and demand of us a reasonable work-life balance.

Our families deserve that we start fighting for it now.

And we can actually achieve this within a few years if we open our workplace doors wide, inviting all those who were previously kept out to join us and then help them to integrate well, remain inside, and thrive. But the rub is that we currently have two important hurdles situated at the workplace entrance, rendering a large group of people unable to join us, no matter how widely we open the doors. I'll explain.

Hurdle 1. Bias and Prejudice

Diversity, equity, and inclusion (DE&I) has become a mainstream and popular topic in the workplace. Yet, in the United States, most people with disabilities (15 percent of the population) are unemployed and greatly underrepresented at the same organizations that proudly host seminars and write op-eds on inclusion.

Is it a lack of ability or is it prejudice that's keeping people with disabilities, ex-felons, and others out? It's 100 percent the latter. For example, minorities as a group obviously don't lack ability, but they still need to send in twice as many applications as mainstream people do just to get an interview. Prejudice is constantly turning potentially contributing members of our society into financial and "welfare burdens" by keeping them out of the workplace, and that same prejudice then blames them for their absence from the workplace by regarding them as "welfare burdens" to society. That's one challenge we will need to overcome when setting our sights on full inclusion.

Hurdle 2. Feeling Unsafe

Even if we wanted to enable full inclusion in the workplace, most current workplaces lack a basic accommodation (the second hurdle) that keeps out many of those trying to get in. This missing accommodation would be easier to see and appreciate if it were a physical one like a ramp, but it's not. It's an emotional accommodation, hence the difficulty in spotting it. But it's as effective at keeping people out of the workplace as it is at lowering the productivity, engagement, and work well-being of many of those currently in it. Our workplaces need to become emotionally healthy and safe for the people working there, and alas they are far from it.

Here are some upsetting stats for you. Regrettably, the modern workplace holds its employees' feelings in very little regard with over 50 percent of US employees feeling unhappy at their jobs. Even worse, the modern workplace is a literal hotbed of bullying with 66 percent of Americans reporting having been bullied at work, while a Glassdoor survey reveals that 61 percent of US employees have personally witnessed or experienced discrimination in the workplace.[7] As we shall see, harassment, bias, and bigotry are deeply embedded in our workplace culture.

NEGLECTING THE VERY THING THAT MAKES US HUMAN: OUR EMOTIONS

Even though the modern workplace goes to great lengths to cater to people's physical needs, it does a remarkably poor job when it comes to their emotional needs. Being shouted at and belittled by a superior causes much emotional pain and is always awful, and the fact that it might happen while you're sitting in a tastefully decorated meeting room is of little consolation. So too does being sexually harassed or bullied cause much emotional pain, even if it occurs on the way to the lavish corporate cafeteria or the new ice cream machine.

You might have noticed yourself that many employers usually neglect to flag "being harassed" or "being publicly humiliated" in their work contracts as "potentially damaging work hazards." There are many among us who cannot psychologically tolerate the cold, uncaring, and at times violent and cruel corporate culture that has all too often become the norm, and they are consequently de facto barred from the workplace by a large emotional barrier. In fact, some CEOs are worshipped in the media as folk heroes for their innovative companies and products while their bullying, harassing, and at times actual cruelty to their colleagues are known but overlooked or intentionally covered up.[8] Since when do individuals' talents entitle them to treat all the people around them like dirt, while causing untold human emotional suffering? Did these people's job descriptions say: "Ability to inflict emotional stress and abuse—a must!"?

Social justice in the workplace will be achieved when large corporations' workforces accurately represent the true diversity of the communities in which they're based. Corporations need to stop talking the talk of inclusion and need to start walking the walk by opening their doors to *all* unemployment underdogs.

DEFINING *EMPLOYMENT UNDERDOGS*

The term *underdog* is American and originates from nineteenth-century dogfights. The winning dog was called the "top dog," and the loser or expected loser was called the "underdog." In modern times, the term *underdogs* usually refers to those who are predicted to lose in a struggle or contest for one of two reasons: because they are initially deemed as lesser or because they are victims of injustice or persecution.

I define *employment underdogs* as those who have to work harder than mainstream people when it comes to finding a job, getting it, keeping it, and succeeding at it in order to enjoy the same success, regardless of their personal merits. Employment underdogs as a group are no lesser than others in any regard *other* than the opportunities they are afforded in the workplace.

Many groups and individuals fall into the category: single moms, religious minorities, victims of injustice, people who are viewed as different from the mainstream, people with a different sexual orientation, people with a different ethnicity, people with low self-confidence, ex-cons and felons, and basically anyone who feels self-doubt regarding their current capacity to fit in and succeed in the workplace.

Researchers have found that 50 percent of interviewers think that candidates can be eliminated from consideration due to the way they dressed, acted, or walked through the door.[9]

Companies place a premium on people who are confident, perform well under stress, learn quickly, and are capable of leaving all of their life problems at the door to the office. Looking and dressing well, having the right accent, and commanding great people skills are also highly regarded. People who are different, slower, less confident, and less attractive are less sought after, less chosen when screened, and less catered to during onboarding and day-to-day operations. When it comes to the workplace, they are often considered underdogs, or in their minds, they feel like underdogs.

In brief, underdogs are a very large group of people who, in the workplace, are often confronted with various degrees of prejudice, and they feel, or are often viewed as slightly, or greatly, less likely to succeed.

EMPLOYMENT UNDERDOG DISCLAIMER

Many employment underdogs are unaware of the added difficulties they face in the workplace. They don't regard themselves as such, nor are they even aware of their underdog status. Underdogs can be amazingly talented and successful, and they can even feel superior and act with annoying hubris. You wouldn't necessarily know that you are earning less than your male counterpart because of your gender or that you were not invited for an interview because of your ethnicity.

My definition has nothing to do with actual merit, capabilities, or success. But whether they realize it or not, most members of nonmainstream groups don't enjoy a level playing field in the workplace, and for some, this disadvantage is enough to keep them chronically unemployed with dire implications. Unemployment is a trunk from which many branches of unhappiness emerge: poverty, lack of purpose and dignity, low self-worth, loneliness, isolation, and often, loss of hope.

WHAT TRUE DIVERSITY MEANS

Workforces that represent the true diversity of their communities means, for instance, the following: people with disabilities constitute 15 percent of the population. (Some people with disabilities are institutionalized and are unable to work; however, the vast majority of people with disabilities can and should work.) Correspondingly, people with disabilities should constitute at least 10 percent of the workforce, not 3 percent or less, as they do today in the United States.[10] Similarly, other underdog groups should be represented in the workforce in very similar proportions in which they exist in the community and the greater society.

Furthermore, in order that everybody find a place in the modern-day workplace, including the shy, the anxious, or the emotionally challenged, opening doors will not be enough. In order to knock down the existing emotional barriers, workplaces should become safe places of social caring.

I will argue that we evolved as a species to work within our tribe, with a strong sense of belonging and in a caring environment where everybody contributes. The fact that so many of us, rich and poor, are depressed, anxious, or generally unhappy is because we are social animals. We function best when provided with the daily human warmth that 200,000 years of hunting and gathering within a caring, close-knit tribe got us used to. The same daily human warmth and caring that's so sorely lacking at many of our places of work. Tribes and families are not devoid of fighting, arguing, and shouting, but these feel totally different when you know that at the end of the day you are regarded and cared for as an individual.

In short, social justice in the workplace will be achieved when corporate America and other workplaces actively strive for full inclusion and change their current emotionally detached culture to one of human warmth and caring. The question is, how can such a change transpire? What are the stepping-stones we need to traverse? Is this change practical or even possible? What can each of us do to facilitate the process?

HOW THIS BOOK IS ORGANIZED

In order to answer these questions in the most granular and practical form possible, I've divided this book into three parts.

Part I: The Current Realities and Future Benefits of Diversity, Equity, and Inclusion

In Part I, I'll describe the current state of affairs regarding DE&I, and I'll prove that corporate America is far from upholding the same values they publicly claim to deeply believe in and endeavor to live up to.

You might be surprised how widely their talk and their walk differ and how large their hypocrisy is.

I'll detail the huge financial, social, and individual gains to be had if we succeed at making full inclusion in the workplace a norm, and I will detail the work that large corporations—which typically tout their corporate and social responsibility (CSR) investments—must do to actually get us there. The global Fortune 500 have a combined yearly CSR budget of—wait for it: a staggering $20 billion. I'll tell you how they utilize it regarding the employment of the world's overlooked underdogs.

You might get upset.

To prove that underdogs have as much ability as anyone else, I'll introduce you to a company founded purely in order to serve as a showcase, a proof of concept regarding underdog talent. It is perhaps the only free-market, for-profit company out there that is staffed and managed entirely by people from some of the most overlooked and chronically unemployed underdog groups. People you need to hear about, whose heroics inspire, educate, and amaze while laying to rest any doubts you might have regarding the practicality of wanting everyone to successfully find and keep a job.

Part II: Underdog Challenges and Remedies

In Part II, I'll describe how corporate America's current culture of disregarding people's emotional needs is keeping many employees out and making many of those who do work miserable. I'll explain how employees' emotions should be regarded throughout their employment life cycle and why it is important to do so.

I'll introduce you to a new human resource entity that can greatly contribute to employees' sense of community, and I'll provide new, granular, and easy-to-use insights and recommendations regarding screening, training, and onboarding that call into question the relevance of some widely practiced traditional procedures.

I'll explain why the most important term in management is, absurdly, the one least mentioned in managerial theory and practice. I'll prove that abusing power in the workplace has reached epidemic dimensions, and I'll describe the terrible effect such abuse has on more than 50 percent of US employees. I'll detail the psychological processes that transform people who were initially warm and caring into cold, unempathetic, and at times abusive managers, and I'll explain why power abuse is in general so widespread and so impervious to change. And finally, I'll explain how workplace harassment and abuse can, in effect, be significantly curtailed, and where such efforts have been previously successful.

If you have ever been harassed, belittled, or bullied at work (most have), you might be awarded some clarity, and hopefully comfort, from understanding the psychology involved.

Part III: Getting from Here to There

After covering what specifically must change in our workplaces how, why, and by whom, in Part III I'll acquaint you with the concept of Reserved Employment for the Opportunity Deprived (REOD). I will introduce you to a large and truly amazing company that is far ahead of the rest of the corporate world in achieving actual diversity, equity, inclusion, and social responsibility. Far, far ahead.

I'll then describe what you, and every person who really craves social justice, can do to help get us there. It's not a big ask at all, and it's well within people's comfort zones. Power doesn't just reside in the workplace. It also resides within us as individuals, family members, and friends, and it's time we collectively harnessed it. We need to stand behind the core value described in the US Declaration of Independence, upheld by the charters of the United Nations and the

European Union—the one about everyone's equality and unalienable rights.

Throughout, I'll present a plethora of academic studies, surveys, and factoids that validate my claims, together with practical proof designed to convince you that at long last, we have a real opportunity to make significant inroads toward social justice, as long as we combine our efforts and focus them on the workplace. It will make all our lives better, richer, and healthier, and it will save countless lives and end much human suffering and misery.

This book is about the road we should take and the part people need to play in order for to get us there. I have dedicated the last 20 years of my life preparing arguments, collecting research, and literally building proof, trying to eliminate any reason or excuse anyone might have for hesitation or uncertainty regarding full inclusion. We have everything we need to win this fight, and now is the time to start it.

Everyone loves a good underdog story, right? You'll be reading a few you've never heard before. I have always believed that all humans are born with equal rights. I have always believed that the strength of communities is measured by the treatment they afford their weakest, and I believe many share these beliefs. The road to social justice starts in the workplace. It's a battle for our excluded brother and sister humans, as well as for our own emotional health and well-being. It's a battle we can and shall win—with underdogs.

PART I

THE CURRENT REALITIES AND FUTURE BENEFITS OF DIVERSITY, EQUITY, AND INCLUSION

1

~~~~~

Diversity, Equity, and Inclusion: Corporate America's Biggest Con Job

Only 3.2 percent of companies on the Fortune 500 list
release the race and gender data of their employees.[1]

*I*nclusion has become a trendy word when it comes to the workplace. Most large companies have inclusion officers, many publish articles about their inclusion practices, and diversity, equity, and inclusion (DE&I) is all the rage in HR research and popular publications nowadays. Amazon sells over 4,000 books under the diversity and inclusion topic alone, many written in just the past few years. Any supporter of DE&I should be filled with optimism at the stellar rise in popularity the idea of inclusion in the workplace seems to be enjoying.

And yet the current use of the term *inclusion* is highly problematic, and I fear that in practice, it actually serves to foster the opposite—exclusion. The *Cambridge Dictionary* defines *inclusion* as, "the act of including someone or something as part of a group." According to this definition, if a large (theoretical) company had no Black or brown people working for them at all, and they decided to hire a few Black people (but not brown people), they would be considered "inclusive." After all they are "*including* some Black people as part of their group," albeit while continuing to leave brown people out.

Viewing these efforts, Black people and others might think that this (theoretical) company is inclusive: "Look they're opening their doors to people of color." But, in fact, this theoretical company is operating with pure prejudice and bias. They continue their practice of barring their doors to certain groups just because of their race and ethnicity or their background or beliefs. They continue to disregard people's personal merits and capabilities, and they judge applicants mainly according to the group they belong to. They've just stopped doing it to Black people. In this example, it's easy to see that this theoretical company doesn't practice inclusion at all. Rather they practice the complete opposite—exclusion.

IT TAKES A LOT OF PEOPLE TO SUCCESSFULLY EXCLUDE

If you think about it, exclusion needs to run deep in order for it to become a companywide phenomenon. Many HR people and managers throughout the company need to share and/or act upon the same core biases and beliefs regarding certain groups in order for it to succeed. It necessitates extensive shared prejudice that must be rooted in the corporate culture. I'll illustrate.

Imagine that a large company decides that they wish to minimize the number of Muslim employees. What would that company need to do in order to successfully limit the number of Muslim applicants and new employees? They would need to possess a company culture that accepted silent undercurrents of exclusion and bias toward Muslim individuals. The bias undercurrents wouldn't need to be strong at all. Subtle cues conveying satisfaction when hiring mainstream applicants as opposed to indifference when hiring Muslims would be enough to gradually increase Muslim exclusion. Some HR people might have ingrained prejudice toward Muslim individuals, but many others will flow with the company's unspoken preferences. Without such companywide exclusion undercurrents and subtle cues, some HR people might just go ahead and *mistakenly* hire Muslims who seem to have potential.

In corporate America, exclusion is seldom an individual's preference or folly. Rather, it's institutionalized—that is, it's in the culture. For a large company to have very few Black people or women in senior positions or very few ex-cons or very few immigrants working for them, it takes the tacit coordination of many people in the company. It requires an exclusive company undertone and culture that encourages hiring mainly from mainstream groups, rather than from minority groups. Similarly, to have women significantly underrepresented in senior management entails active widespread, but often unspoken misogyny.

Get Rid of the Bouncer! Understanding the Dynamics of Inclusion

To achieve real social justice in the workplace, for corporate America to become truly inclusive, including "someone" or "some groups" isn't good enough. We have to include everyone and all groups. In the past few years, various companies have tried to convince us of the sincerity of their inclusion efforts by opening their doors to specific groups. Unfortunately, "We're hiring Black people" or "We're promoting women" or "We just opened our gates to this or that group" just serves to punctuate and consolidate exclusion. By allowing companies to "focus" their "inclusion" efforts on one group at a time while leaving their doors barred to others, we are actively legitimizing the practice of *excluding* various groups and individuals from the workplace.

You either judge people on their own individual merits, or you judge them based on the group they belong to or the place they hail from. If you act upon the latter and exclude *anyone* based on the group they belong to, then it's totally irrelevant which precise group it is that you're excluding. It still makes you biased and your actions prejudiced and exclusive. It's just like stealing—and even if you're stealing from only one group, it's still stealing, and it makes the transgressor a thief.

To put it simply, you can't have a "bouncer" at the door selecting who gets in and who doesn't and claim to be inclusive and diverse, even if you start to limit the bouncer's list of undesirables. You are either inclusive, have no bouncer, and welcome everyone (based on personal merit), or you are exclusive and your bouncers keep certain people out just because of the group they belong to, disregarding completely who they are as individuals. The identity and variety of the excluded is irrelevant. In this sense, *all* lives matter, and *no one* deserves to be harassed.

A Corporation Is Either Fully Inclusive or It's Exclusionary

There is no such thing as partial inclusion, and as long as any one group is excluded from a workplace, that workplace is in actuality exclusive. For a corporation to regard itself as "inclusive" it must be *fully* inclusive. I define *full inclusion* as accepting everyone other than two groups of people: (1) people who are actively paying the price for their crimes and are currently incarcerated, and (2) people whose physical or mental condition is so severe that they are institutionalized and need constant caretaking. The rest of the members of our societies, globally, deserve a place in the job market because deeming any group or members of our society as unworthy, unable, unnoticed, or undeserving is the literal opposite of social justice. And it sure as hell isn't inclusion.

Because I wish to promote a global change regarding the diversity and culture of our workplaces, and before I answer the questions of what changes are needed and how we can achieve them, let's examine the "why." Why should corporate America, our communities, and ourselves be highly motivated and committed to this change? Is it really worth our collective efforts?

DIVERSITY IS GREAT FOR MAXIMIZING PROFIT

Achieving full inclusion in the workplace is a huge social undertaking because, when you look at the DE&I data that is available (much isn't), you'll see so many workplaces that obviously hold biases toward certain groups who are markedly underrepresented in their workforce. Any corporation wishing to change such widespread prejudice will face a lengthy battle that will demand enormous effort, grit, and perseverance. Many challenges and objections need to be faced and overcome, and many preconceptions and biases need to be addressed and put to rest.

It truly is an immense task, and its undertaking will demand serious motivation and commitment to see it through. Social justice might be a strong enough motivator when it comes to the currently unemployed and their families who crave inclusion, but they aren't the ones who need to undergo profound change. That's the job of large corporations and employers. And for that to be contemplated in a capitalistic profit-driven economy, *it's crucial that the financial benefits to employers justify the immense efforts required.*

After all, we are basically asking employers to forgo their hiring strategy of searching only for the best and brightest mainstream candidates, and instead we're asking them to become fully diverse. Often that will entail hiring people who look different, come from different backgrounds, or have been afforded lesser schooling.

Some might come in at an initial lower level of performance, or with weaker initial capabilities, some might even be difficult to employ for various reasons and need various accommodations. This is an ask that does seem to go against sound financial reason because, after all, the more uniform people are, the easier it is to train and manage them. Can diversity in any way be congruent with maximizing profits? Is it really financially worth their while?

Well, happily, full inclusion and employee diversity turns out to be great for business, while neglecting diversity efforts could actually be akin to playing with fire, and it could cause company profits to suffer an excruciating third-degree burn.

WHY FULL INCLUSION GREATLY FACILITATES A COMPANY'S BOTTOM LINE

There are three main factors that will deeply and positively affect organizations that choose the full inclusion route: elevated consumer support, elevated employee engagement, and lowered employee attrition. It's quite shocking what a huge impact on an organization's bottom line these three can have. It can literally make or break them.

Consumer Power and Support

Consumers over the years have always had the ability to vote with their feet (wallet), and with the rise of the internet and social media, consumers can now also greatly influence what other people buy. Correspondingly, in the past few years, many consumers developed a growing sensitivity to social issues and began advocating for corporations and products that register high on matters of social justice while punishing transgressors. As a result, more and more people are using the internet not only to uncover the true worth of a company's products but also to uncover the true worth of the company's values and social responsibilities.

The *2018 Edelman Earned Brand Global Report* found that 47 percent of consumers in the United States were belief-driven buyers, meaning that "they choose, switch, avoid, or boycott a brand based on its stand on social issues."[2] One year later, in 2019, the number of belief-driven buyers in the United States rose to 59 percent, a 25 percent increase in just one year. Similar trends are underway in many other countries.

Given the rise of belief-driven consumers, any corporation that is forthcoming and fully transparent regarding the makeup of its workforce and that proudly boasts a team that truly reflects the diversity of the community will garnish tremendous consumer support. And the more positive benchmarks of this kind consumers have, the more they will punish businesses that are not transparent or inclusive. Corporations worldwide are learning that various social injustices that they could get away with not so many years ago are nowadays more noticeable—and are unacceptable in the eyes of many of their customers.

Clearly, we're in the age of belief-driven buyers, and brands that don't factor in social issues accordingly do so at their own peril. In fact, brands know this, and most put much effort into "trying to look the part" by publicly applauding DE&I values and spotlighting their relevant inclusion efforts.

Employee Engagement

There are many definitions of *employee engagement*, but in essence it speaks about how employees feel (emotionally) at their work and the amount of effort they are willing to put in over the long term. The higher employees' engagement, the more productive, loyal, and caring about their workplace they will be. The reason employee engagement has become such a crucial metric for organizations is financial. The differences in productivity and profits between organizations that have high employee engagement and those with low employee engagement is no less than dramatic.

Gallup's tenth employee engagement meta-analysis examined employee engagement and performance data from more than 100,000 teams to evaluate the connection between employee engagement and key business outcomes. When compared with business units in the bottom quartile of engagement, those in the top quartile realized improvements in the following areas:

- 41 percent reduction in absenteeism

- 17 percent increase in productivity

- 10 percent increase in customer ratings

- 20 percent increase in sales

- 21 percent greater profitability

Gallup summarized the importance of employee engagement to a corporation's bottom line as follows: "Simply put, engaged employees produce better business outcomes than other employees do—across industries, company sizes and nationalities, and in good economic times and bad."[3]

DE&I efforts have been proven to raise employee engagement[4] and have a wide positive effect in this regard because in order to become fully inclusive and succeed at employing underdogs, most of an employer's current employees will need to become part of their overall inclusion efforts. Inclusion demands building a culture of equality as well as much employee coordination (as we saw, the similar ingredients are needed for successful exclusion). Consequently, many existing employees will be needed to actively participate in the organization's social responsibility efforts. When the rank and file have an active part in these efforts, their own investment of energy in the welfare of the less fortunate will create both happiness (being kind to others promotes happiness) and a deeper sense of community and belonging, which in turn will promote their own sense of security. After all, "if my employer is investing so much caring and effort in order to employ underdogs from the community, then they are obviously caring employers and will put in the same effort for me."

Perhaps even more importantly, such endeavors add a deep sense of social purpose to organizations that don't intrinsically have one (financial institutions, for instance), all of which greatly contribute to employees' overall engagement.[5]

Employees' desire for a sense of purpose is surprisingly strong. In a recent survey by BetterUp, 9 out of 10 employees were willing to trade a substantial amount of their lifetime earnings for greater meaning and purpose at work.[6] When asked what percent of their earnings they were willing to trade for purpose, the average was 23 percent, which is staggering. It's actually more than we spend on housing (21 percent of our income[7]). We seem to crave purpose at our jobs more than we do a roof over our heads.

Stockholders Have Been Officially Dethroned

Just 25 years ago, companies believed that 100 percent of their purpose was to maximize profits for shareholders, according to a 1997 formal statement of "corporate purpose" put together by senior representatives of 200 of America's leading companies. "The paramount duty of management and of boards of directors is to the corporation's stockholders," the group declared. "The interests of other stakeholders are relevant as a derivative of the duty to stockholders."

Nowadays, corporations are fully cognizant of the importance of having a strong social purpose rather than exclusively striving for maximum profit. As reported by *Fortune*, things have changed.[8] In 2019, a similar group of corporate senior representatives announced a new purpose for corporations, and quite a different one at that. The statement, *Fortune* reported, is 300 words long, and shareholders aren't mentioned until word 250. Instead, the statement refers to creating "value for customers," "investing in employees," fostering "diversity and inclusion," "dealing fairly and ethically with suppliers," "supporting the communities in which we work," and "protect[ing] the environment."

Lower Employee Attrition

Financial gains can also be achieved through lower levels of employee attrition. The rule of thumb is that it costs between 30 to 60 percent of an employee's annual salary to replace the employee and even more for managerial positions.[9] In many cases, once underdogs make it, they often become the employer's best and most loyal employees, the stable backbone of the organization. They turn out to be a core of loyal, appreciative, engaged employees who stay for the long term, believing in and fighting for the same company that believed in and fought for them. In contrast, the top talent that came for the perks often leaves when they get better offers.

The Gallup survey cited earlier demonstrates the dramatic effect engagement has on employee attrition. In low-turnover organizations, the business units in the higher quartile of employee engagement enjoyed 59 percent less turnover than those in the lowest quartile, and in high-turnover organizations, those with engaged employees had 24 percent less turnover than organizations with low employee engagement.

These financial considerations are huge, and they greatly exceed the expenses involved in becoming a fully inclusive organization— and they should definitely create enough positive financial motivation for any organization that wonders if it's worth the effort. But in my mind, the real kicker for executives and veteran employees is emotional, not financial. Telling your kids that you earned a bonus is fun. Telling your kids that you saved a person's life, that you helped an army vet or an older person who had sat at home unemployed for years find a job, make new friends, feel wanted and worthy—now that's a feeling almost as powerful as the one you'll get when you see the pride in your family's eyes at the telling.

In summary, companies that remain exclusive will probably face costly increases in employee attrition, and they risk facing a progressive and scary decline in their customers' support and patronage. On the other hand, it's obvious that companies that endeavor to become fully inclusive experience a wide range of critical financial benefits.

Potential financial rewards can reach double-digit increases in sales, productivity, and overall profit as a result of elevated social purpose and employee engagement alone, while increased consumer support can push those figures up even more. And it's not just employers. Our communities too will reap many financial, social, and humanistic gains from full inclusion.

Why Full Inclusion Greatly Improves Our Communities

Employing chronically unemployed people contributes to the economy directly because their labor provides additional goods or services, thus growing the market, and because they themselves spend their wages buying goods and services thus growing the market even more.

In addition, full inclusion in employment results in savings in welfare services, disability and welfare pensions, training and professional courses for unemployed people, medication and medical costs, and lost work days of nonpaid caretaking by family members. All of these savings could serve to finance significant national improvements in infrastructure, health, and education. We could demolish the daycare centers for the unemployed and build parks, plant trees, and contribute to our community's overall sustainability.

Full Inclusion Benefits to Communities

The benefits to workplaces and communities would make us stronger in additional ways because "the strength of a chain is indeed determined by the strength of its weakest link." We humans are very much social creatures, and strengthening our weakest link strengthens the whole fabric of society. A society in which substantial percentages of the population do not contribute weakens the whole. Viewing all members of society as potential assets and enabling all members of society to contribute strengthens the whole.

From my experience, watching a person with disabilities perform on a par with people without disabilities can sometimes even inspire and increase general motivation and performance. A general increase in inclusion practices also means less poverty, a stronger sense of community, fewer people on the streets, and a stronger collective feeling of belonging while promoting social responsibility and true equality. We will end up with a richer, stronger society that includes and cares for all its members' feelings of security, happiness, and well-being.

Full Inclusion Benefits to Individuals

For chronically unemployed people and their families, having a place to go in the morning, a job, and people waiting for you is akin to leaving prison where a life sentence was unjustly being served. It ends social isolation, elevates feelings of self-worth and self-confidence, greatly facilitates physical as well as emotional health, and generally makes people's lives so much happier and fulfilling. It is the biggest, individual, positive game changer possible. It is true social justice.

I've stated that large organizations have enough financial motivation to undergo change and become fully inclusive. In fact, it seems that not only do they indeed have substantial financial motivation to do so but they also have an allocated a budget for social endeavors. Many large corporations consistently put aside annual budgets to finance their efforts to "give back" to the community, efforts called *corporate social responsibility* (CSR), and these budgets are huge! It's comforting to know that large corporations widely and publicly acknowledge their responsibilities toward the communities they operate out of, and it's interesting to see how they live up to these responsibilities.

EXECUTIVE TEAM DIVERSITY IMPROVES FINANCIAL PERFORMANCE

A 2020 survey of more than 1,000 large companies in 15 countries by the consulting firm McKinsey & Company provided substantial evidence that diversity in the executive suite improves financial performance.[10]

According to the survey, "Companies with more than 30 percent women executives were more likely to outperform companies where the percentage ranged from 10 to 30, and in turn these companies were more likely to outperform those with even fewer women executives, or none at all."

In the case of ethnic and cultural diversity, the business-case findings were equally compelling. In 2019, companies in the top quartile of executive team diversity outperformed those in the bottom quartile by 36 percent in profitability.

Nonetheless, the survey also showed that diversity gains have been small since the firm's original 2014 study. Female representation on executive teams in the United States and United Kingdom rose from 15 percent in 2014 to 20 percent in 2019. However, "across our global data set, for which our data starts in 2017, gender diversity moved up just one percentage point—to 15 percent from 14 percent—in 2019," McKinsey reported.

Representation of ethnic minorities on US and UK executive teams stood at only 13 percent in 2019, up from just 7 percent in 2014. Globally, the proportion was 14 percent in 2019, up from 12 percent in 2017.

THE 2020 GLOBAL FORTUNE 500 AND GIVING

By 2013 the combined annual CSR budget of the global Fortune (GF) 500 was just under $20 billion,[11] a sum equivalent to the national annual budget of countries like Bulgaria, Uruguay, or Kenya. How should the global Fortune 500 best maximize their social impact with such vast resources?

Common sense dictates that because large companies are first and foremost large employers, one of their primary social responsibilities should be employment. And while these companies do hire the top talent in their local communities, most are not giving anything to the local community by doing so—they're just taking. After all, it's not the top dogs who struggle to find work. It's those whose prospects are impeded by corporate culture, bias, and narrow-mindedness—it's the underdogs.

Communities' Unaddressed Employment Needs and Corporations' Real Employment Responsibilities

The more people in a community who have jobs, the greater the benefit to the community. The problem is that it's usually more challenging to screen and employ underdogs because the disadvantages that have sidelined them might require employers to invest more resources and effort, at least initially, in order to employ them successfully. For example, veterans might have posttraumatic stress disorder (PTSD) and other issues that can make social integration more challenging for them. Ex-cons broke certain laws, so it might take time to build mutual trust in an organization employing them.

But if we really want full inclusion, if we really want everyone to be able to join the job market, whose responsibility is it to hire those who require more effort to successfully employ? Who has the resources to invest in the weaker members of our community? The necessary personnel, the necessary job openings? The local mom-and-pop grocery stores or the large corporations? It's the corporations, of course. That's why their budgets fall under the "corporate *social* responsibility" heading. The same logic dictates, therefore, that the larger the business, the more they should challenge themselves to employ those in the community who require the most initial effort. The richest employers should be the ones to employ the most challenging of the employment underdogs because it is they who have the resources to do so—and "with great power (resources) comes great responsibility."

Large employers have substantial financial motivations to promote their own inclusiveness. They have a social responsibility to address their community's employment needs by employing those who are more difficult to employ, and they have large CSR budgets at their disposal to do so. They also generally have large collective IQs with abundant problem-solving capabilities. Clearly, they have all the necessary ingredients to give back and really change the diversity of the modern workplace for the better. In short, they have the responsibility, motivation, capability, and funding! Unfortunately, when it comes to giving in this regard, most not only fail but they fail miserably.

The Truth About Giving

Give a man a fish, feed him for a day.
Teach him to fish, feed him for a lifetime.
—Lao Tzu

Lao Tzu's proverb is often used to highlight the effectiveness of giving, distinguishing between reducing a problem momentarily and solving it for the long run. But it can also be used to highlight the actions and sincerity of the giver, by distinguishing between two very different kinds of giving: *superficial* and *profound*.

Superficial Giving

Giving a person a fish requires very little effort or sacrifice. It just takes a minute and is given from one's surplus, so I call this kind of no-effort giving *superficial giving*. Superficial giving is selfish in nature because often the unspoken narrative behind it is in actuality 100 percent self-serving. For example, a company might say this:

> We write a check, takes two minutes, we can afford it easily, and it'll help us out in lots of ways. It will lower the threat of potential outside criticism regarding our social responsibilities, we get to feel all fuzzy and warm about ourselves, we look good helping the community and get great PR. Plus, we reduce any guilt feelings any of us might feel regarding the truly massive difference between our own personal wealth and finances and the financial struggles of many in the community.

Corporate superficial giving isn't aimed at alleviating community suffering. Its goals are to stave off potential criticism and allow senior management to feel noble and magnanimous with minimum effort. To me, corporate superficial giving is akin to an executive passing a hungry unemployed underdog on the way to their car, and tossing them a fish. "Here, food for a day" they say as they get into the car with a self-congratulatory smirk as they brag to their driver, "Giving is in my nature."

Maimonides (1138–1204), a famous medieval philosopher, was also concerned with various types of giving, and he described eight levels of giving based on values and honoring the feelings of the recipient. The least noble kind of giving, level 8, is described as giving only following coercion and with a "sour countenance." Level 7 is giving much less than you can afford; level 6 is giving generously, but only after you were asked; level 5 is giving before you were asked; level 4 is giving when you do not know the recipient's identity; level 3 is giving when the recipient doesn't know the identity of the giver; and level 2 is giving via a third party where the identity of the giver and recipient are unknown to each other. Level 1, the most noble kind of giving according to Maimonides, is when the gift is such that it enables the recipient to become self-sufficient. In essence, the gift of teaching someone to fish.

Corporate America's giving is often PR driven, it's much less than they can afford, and they make sure everyone knows about it. In the realm of noble giving, they are practically on the bottom rung (other than the "sour countenance" part).

Profound Giving

On the other hand, teaching people to fish is practically the complete opposite form of giving. It could take years, not minutes or hours, and it demands the investment of much personal effort, patience, and care. It requires the teacher to constantly interact with the relevant people in order to help them master an important skill that has eluded them to date: fishing or providing for one's self and family. It's far from easy, and it's often laborious, but it's a labor fueled by values, responsibility, love, and compassion. I call this kind of giving *profound giving* because its outcomes for the benefactors as well as the givers are life changing and tenfold.

Back to the Fortune 500 companies and their billions of CSR dollars. None of them are fishing companies so they don't really provide the needy with fish. Their *main* social responsibility to the community should be in the realm of employment as that is the best way to teach a community to fish. But looking around the CSR landscape, one notices that very few fishing lessons are actually being offered. Albeit, there is a lot of superficial giving and check writing, but upsettingly, there also seems to be quite a bit of cheating going on as well, as, for example, in the case of Google and disability inclusion—as described below.

INCLUSION WASHING: TALKING INSTEAD OF DOING

When it comes to donating money to causes related to people with disabilities, Google is generous. In 2016 Google.org, awarded $20 million to 30 (disability-related) nonprofits charged with developing technologies ranging from open-source electric wheelchairs to multilingual keyboards you can control with eye-tracking technology. However, when it comes to employment, it is unclear from Google's annual reports how many people with disabilities *actually work* for Google. In fact, in some countries where it is mandatory for employers to hire people with disabilities, Google extracts itself from this commitment using legal loopholes to shirk its social responsibilities.[12]

Indeed, Google and many other brands actively divert our collective gaze away from their profound social responsibility of employing the community's underdogs, and they turn our gaze toward their superficial giving practices of a few senior executives handing out some fish or touting the inclusiveness of their products.

Disability:IN is a large global nonprofit that claims their Disability Equality Index is "the most comprehensive benchmarking tool for disability inclusion."[13] Google is proud to boast that it scored 100/100 on the Disability Equality Index as do many other large corporations. A perfect score, not one thing wrong, not one point taken off. Google apparently epitomizes disability inclusion, the highest and furthest a company can go, at least according to Disability:IN and "the most comprehensive benchmarking tool for disability inclusion."

I was curious to know what percentage of Disability:IN's 100 percent score reflects *actually* employing people with disabilities. Not that I want to nitpick, but if an organization is getting graded on disability inclusion, it does seem reasonable that the organization's actual inclusion practice—the percentage of people with disabilities de facto working for them—should be a leading metric in the overall score, shouldn't it? Well, it turns out that the contribution to the overall score of actually employing people with disabilities is 10 percent. Yup, that's it, a measly 10 percent. That means that companies can get 90 percent without employing any people with disabilities at all—on a disability inclusion index. Is it just me, or does that seem a bit—naughty?

Forbes too promotes Google's disability employment practices, as in a 2017 article titled "Accenture, EY, Google, Microsoft and Other Leaders Find Great Value in Employees with Disabilities," by Paolo Gaudiano.[14]

Here's the truth: Making your products accessible to people with disabilities isn't disability inclusion—it's actually sound business. It enables you to grow your potential client base and sales by 15 to 20 percent—which is the percentage of people with disabilities in the population. Making your products and facilities accessible to people with disabilities is also mandatory in many countries, so doing so simply constitutes following the law and avoiding fines. It's not voluntary disability inclusion at all, and countries mandate it by law precisely because until they did, many corporations didn't bother to make their products and facilities accessible because of cost issues. Companies shouldn't get a disability inclusion rating of 100 percent if all they do is provide access. The main criteria *must* be actual employment. Disability:IN should in fact be viewed as a standard for expediting sales and revenue off people with disabilities, rather than a measure of workplace inclusion.

Getting back to Google. The company states that 15 percent of the people in the world have a disability. Therefore, with a workforce of 100,000 people worldwide, coupled with an apparent deep appreciation of the value people with disabilities bring and in view of their perfect score on the Disability Equality Index (they did get the full 10 percent for employment), one would expect Google to have at least 15,000 employees with disabilities (15 percent) working for them or thereabouts. You could point out that some people with disabilities are indeed very challenging to hire, so perhaps 10,000 employees with disabilities would be a fairer benchmark. OK, does Google have 10,000 employees with disabilities? No, it does not even come close. Only 6 percent of Google employees (6,000 employees) identify as having a disability.[15]

This is especially frustrating because if Google truly aimed for and eventually achieved equality in underdog employment, the company would inspire not only other huge players in the high-tech industry but also corporations and organizations in all industries across the world. Google has the international standing and potential to become the global DE&I's knight in shining armor. However, to date, I'm sad to say, when it comes to CSR and employment, Google, as do so many others, mainly takes the route of superficial giving. They seem to be strong on the disability inclusion talk, but when it comes to the walk, they and others seem to have a disability themselves . . .

It Takes Only One

Imagine the chain reaction if the head of a global company like Google, Sodexo, or Alibaba, backed by the board of directors, announced that the company was starting their own full inclusion initiative, making it a policy at all their sites to hire numerous employees from the ranks of the chronically unemployed. As it progressed to full inclusion, the company would be heralded as an international hero; belief-driven consumers would flock to buy their products; and their employees' engagement would soar, driven by the renewed vigor a strong sense of social purpose brings.

Investors would stand in line to buy their stock, sending the price soaring. The company would immediately become the social inclusion benchmark that all other corporations would be judged by.

How long would it take other large organizations to follow suit? Employees would demand that their employers join the full inclusion trend. The power of the internet and belief-driven consumers would add a huge amount of outside pressure to these demands. First one and then another global company would follow suit, creating a ripple effect that would sweep the globe. We need just one hero, one global business leader, willing to lead the company and the world to a future of full inclusion and social justice.

The Underdog Ranks Are Swelling

The emergence of Covid-19 has resulted in many people losing their jobs or going on prolonged furloughs. Eighteen months after the outbreak of the pandemic, millions of Americans were still missing from the job market, with many of these people and others rethinking their post-covid careers.[16] As the days turned into weeks and months, many people lost confidence, and they are likely to have their future job seeking efforts hindered by their current emotional state, thus joining the ranks of the employment underdogs.

On a scale of unemployment challenges, people who in their recent past have successfully held a job are easier to reintroduce to the job market. But what about those who have never worked? Or those who can work only a paltry number of hours a week because of medical reasons? Or those who barely speak the language? Does full inclusion apply to them too? Do we really have to make a point of getting everyone into the job market? Why not start with the "easier cases" and gradually work our way from there? Would that not work better?

In fact, the complete opposite is true. For a corporation to successfully become fully inclusive, its leaders must first convince their current employees (recruiters, managers, team members—those who do the hiring, training, and onboarding) that they are sincere in their wish to uphold the value of equality and to become fully inclusive.

However, after years of inclusion rhetoric that simply masked the realities of exclusion, wage gaps, and prejudice, their employees plum won't believe that this time, their companies actually mean it. The only way to convince employees is to display real and total commitment. Following decades of big diversity talk, with miniscule diversity progress, anything less than a full commitment will be regarded as token and even deceitful by both employees and customers. Like it or not, corporate America has some serious heart-searching to do and crucial DE&I amendments to make.

2

~~~~~~

Equality Hypocrisy and the Challenging Road to Equality Integrity

*There are fewer women among chief executives of
Fortune 500 companies than there are men named John.*[1]

In a world of belief-driven customers, any self-respecting brand
must at least pay lip service to DE&I from a values standpoint.

> **IBM:** IBM is committed to creating a diverse environment and
> is proud to be an equal opportunity employer. All qualified ap-
> plicants will receive consideration for employment without
> regard to race, color, religion, gender, gender identity or expres-
> sion, sexual orientation, national origin, genetics, disability, age,
> or veteran status.[2]

Some brands go beyond values, explaining in addition that inclusion and diversity are paramount to the overall success of their
business:

Apple: Because to create products that serve everyone, we believe in including everyone.[3]

Coca-Cola: We champion diversity by building a workforce as diverse as the consumers we serve. Because the more perspectives we have, the better decisions we make.[4]

Google: At Google, we don't just accept difference—we celebrate it, we support it, and we thrive on it for the benefit of our employees, our products and our community.[5]

So, it seems that other than the financial benefits I previously detailed, large organizations on their own add two powerful motivators that drive them to become fully inclusive: enhancing their businesses (inclusion enables them to better understand consumers, to build better products, to make better decisions) and upholding the core value of equality. I believe the first, but I have some serious doubts regarding their commitment to the second. Are these value statements sincere? Are these brands indeed motivated to really uphold these values and do they and others truly act on them, or are they simply giving them self-serving lip service? Let's examine how corporations currently uphold their core value of equality.

UPHOLDING THE VALUE OF EQUALITY IN CORPORATE AMERICA

Let's look at the gender wage gap as an example of easy-to-fix inequality. In general, women in the United States make about 80 percent of men doing similar work, but when it comes to women of color, these discrepancies grow. Black women and Latinas lose, on average, more than $1 million over their lifetime to the wage gap, an utterly staggering amount if you think about it.[6] If I were a Black or Latina woman hearing this for the first time, I don't know if I would be ecstatic learning about my potential for an increase in salary or furious that corporate America was getting richer by shortchanging me.

Happily, companies that believe in equality and want to make sure that they don't discriminate against women when it comes to wages can easily conduct a pay equity audit. You might think that some companies are apprehensive of conducting such an audit, fearing that fixing any found inequality will be extremely costly to the company. However, a 2019 study found that the total remediation cost to organizations adds up to 0.1 to 0.3 percent of their total salary budget, a mere smidgen.

You might think that such a simple audit coupled with such an apparent low cost of remediation ("apparent" in that companies finding mostly *small* wage gaps were probably more likely to report than those with large wage gaps) most companies would pounce on the opportunity to finally pay women workers their fair share. Makes sense, right? Well, unfortunately, it makes sense just to us. Of the 922 largest public companies in the United States, most of whom endlessly tout their commitment to gender equality, 78 percent haven't even bothered to conduct such a survey in the past five years.[7]

Corporate America's (Lack of) Values

In the workplace, values, noble as they may be, have always faced one major antagonist: maximum profit. Maximum profit to values is like kryptonite to Superman—it sucks the life right out of them. The closer and larger the monetary gains, the bigger the chance that someone's resolve will inevitably give. After all, untasteful or even slightly immoral is not the same as illegal and can always be justified as "just business."

When companies talk about their values, the unmentioned, ever-present caveat of "as long as it doesn't disrupt our bottom line" causes many in the organizations themselves to be skeptical. The naked truth is that in a vast majority of brands, value statements regarding DE&I are PR driven, insincere, and in many cases, by definition downright hypocritical. And at long last, it's starting to get noticed more and more.

Google's and Microsoft's Black and Latinx tech staff has gone up less than 1 percent since 2014.[8]

Management expert Patrick M. Lencioni wrote in *Harvard Business Review:*

> Most values statements are bland, toothless, or just plain dishonest. And far from being harmless, as some executives assume, they're often highly destructive. Empty values statements create cynical and dispirited employees, alienate customers, and undermine managerial credibility. . . . Today, 80 percent of the Fortune 100 tout their values publicly—values that too often stand for nothing but a desire to be au courant or, worse still, politically correct.

Brands that don't publicly presume to pursue equality are by definition bigoted, but at least they're candid. However, brands that publicly speak of equality as one of their core values and yet leave easy-to-fix inequalities in place for years (by avoiding pay equity audits, for example) should not only be considered bigoted but perhaps should also be labeled as "equality hypocritical" brands and exposed as such.

BIGOTRY IS GLOBAL AND A NEMESIS TO EQUALITY

But before we start boycotting equality hypocritical brands, in all fairness, it has to be said that when it comes to equality and hypocrisy, it's not just brands. It's us. It's all of us. We're all equality hypocrites, and we always have been. By and large, we humans—as nations, as societies, as brands, and as individuals—have horrible track records when it comes to upholding the value of equality. Our bigotry is deep, long lasting, and global in scope.

Equality Hypocrisy in Individuals

Equality hypocrisy arises when equality values aren't applied equally, or when principles and their application are systematically discrepant. A 2015 study published in the journal *Peace and Conflict* found "clear evidence of equality hypocrisy in most of us as individuals, because people were less willing to endorse equal rights for specific groups than they were for all groups."[9] In the study, a large majority of subjects (84 percent) initially claimed they valued equality for all groups in general. But when asked if they held this value regarding specific groups, fewer than 65 percent considered it important to satisfy the needs of Black people, fewer than 60 percent considered it important for Muslims, and fewer than 50 percent considered it important for homosexual people.

In other words, people were comfortable with saying, "Sure everybody should be treated equally . . . but perhaps not the gays or Muslims." It's the same bigotry that caused some (misogynous) people to not understand why the movie *Borat* is a comedy. (The character Borat is a primitive, misogynous man who "knows" that women are cognitively much inferior to men.) It's not surprising that the study found that "this [equality] hypocrisy was manifested [both] at the [individual and] aggregate level characterizing society as a whole."

But how does this discrepancy evolve in so many of us? Why do so many of us entertain unfounded biases toward specific groups while affirming our general belief in equality? What are the psychological processes at work?

Only 17 percent of workers support increased recruiting of underrepresented racial and ethnic groups.[10]

There is a discrepancy between how we think of our ideal selves (the person we like to think we are) and how we actually are. Our ideal self believes we are fair and just, so most of us state that, indeed, all people are equal and deserve equal rights. However, our real selves are swayed by many things that influence our actual beliefs and behavior. Certain life experiences, social norms we grew up with, fear of people who are different from us, or even a charismatic figure who influenced us—all can cause subtle biases that become deeply internalized in our psyche. We are often not aware of these gradual processes and their effect on our outlook and beliefs, which makes biases so tricky to tackle, and that's why we so often hear biased statements start with, "I'm not biased but . . ."

Equality Hypocrisy in Societies and Nations

On the one hand, many countries and societies seem to hold the value of equality in the highest regard and have been doing so over a substantial amount of time. It says so in the Declaration of Independence, which was written over 200 years ago; in the Universal Declaration of Human Rights (UDHR), adopted by the General Assembly of the United Nations Organization in 1948 ("All human beings are born free and equal in dignity and rights . . ."); and in the charter of fundamental rights of the European Union from just 2012.[11]

But in fact, there was always a huge divide between nations' rhetoric over equality and their actions. The Declaration of Independence was written while slavery and the lack of voting rights for women were the norm. The UDHR is signed by nations that still today deprive women of basic rights (like voting) or outlaw homosexuality.

The Equality "Talk and Walk" Discrepancy

Globally, we are very consistent regarding our stated, outspoken beliefs in equality. Everyone says they're for equality. We read it in headlines. We hear it in global and national declarations. Democracies are founded on the basis of equality. And large companies claim equality as a core value.

We fight and demonstrate for equality. Leaders and politicians tout equality as a basic and paramount right, and we even have "bad" words for people, like "bigot," "racist," or "prejudiced," who stray from the value of equality. And when it comes to us as individuals, we expect, fight for, and demand equality for ourselves and others. Our talk regarding equality is robust, copious, and decisive.

And yet when it comes to the "walk," our actions, deeds, and outcomes are completely inadequate. In essence, we tolerate and perpetuate inequality. Even people who have suffered a lifetime of marginalization just because they belong to a certain group will often hold prejudiced views of groups that they see as different and inferior.[12] Such biases can stem from an unconscious need to not be at the bottom of the social ladder, a need to feel socially superior, as a response to feeling threatened by that group (no more people on the life raft), or just because we at times need a "bad guy" to take the blame in the narrative of our life. But the fact remains that the discrepancy between our stated beliefs in equality and our actions is often huge and across the board.

The main takeaways from this distressing state of affairs are that when it comes to judging the candor of any company's equality-related agenda or public statements, their words should be regarded with skepticism. In fact, we should totally discard their "talk" and focus solely on their "walk." Our collective, dismal track record and ubiquitous global equality hypocrisy should cause us to view any corporation's DE&I efforts, even those with good intent, as suspect at best.

Corporations that wish to adopt a DE&I strategy based on true equality and integrity must include a few essential components that are vitally required if they wish to uproot the deep skepticism and doubt that years of equality hypocrisy have embedded in our collective psyche.

THE THREE ESSENTIAL COMPONENTS OF CORPORATE AMERICA'S CHALLENGING ROAD TO EQUALITY INTEGRITY

The bigger the discrepancy between words and actions, the bigger the challenge to close the gap. With such large gaps in mind, corporations that wish to truly act upon the value of equality and become fully inclusive must incorporate into their DE&I strategy the following three essential components: bottom-up hiring, transparency, and top-down accountability.

1. Bottom-Up Hiring

A person's integrity can be defined as the extent to which that person acts with loyalty in accordance with their stated values, beliefs, and principles. Corporations that truly wish to transition from equality hypocrisy to equality integrity need to demonstrate their loyalty to their stated values with rigor. They should use their considerable talents, finances, and clout to adopt a DE&I strategy that favors hiring first and foremost from the most excluded groups, those that often face difficulties in the modern corporate culture, those that have been out of a job for years, those that might demand real effort in order to get up to par.

Sincere DE&I strategies should start at the bottom of the unemployment totem, with those who have been overlooked the most, those who have been afforded the least. Anything less will be viewed as the easy way out and a return to their hypocritical ways. If the "employer strongest" don't tend to the "employee weakest," they leave that task to others with fewer resources and lesser chances of success. This is the real social responsibility of corporate America—a responsibility they have been shirking for too long.

2. Transparency

We shouldn't care about current corporate inclusion rhetoric. It's hypocritical. Instead, we must see the corporations' inclusion practices and outcomes in the form of detailed, verifiable data regarding the makeup of their workforce. The larger the corporations, the more responsibility they should shoulder and the more detailed their inclusion reports should be.

Most large corporations' inclusion reports (not many are available) refer to gender, Black people, Asians, and Hispanics. Very little mention is made of other significant employee underdog groups like ex-cons, ex-felons, and people with disabilities.

A 2018 report from the Prison Policy Initiative found that the unemployment rate for formerly incarcerated people is nearly five times higher than the unemployment rate for the general US population.

It is estimated that as of 2019, 24 million Americans (that's just under 10 percent of the adult population in the United States) have a felony in their past—which means many employers will not even consider them for jobs.[13] Accordingly, they have the dubious honor of being one of the most unemployed population groups. Another vastly unemployed group in the United States are people with disabilities of which there are 61 million adults, which is about 26 percent of the adult population. According to the U.S. Department of Labor, only 17.9 percent of people with a disability were employed in 2020.

You may have noticed large variations with data regarding people with disabilities. Some sources like Statista contend that 13 percent of the US population have a disability,[14] and the number provided by the CDC is more than twice that: 26 percent. When it comes to people with disabilities, measuring is a problem. Do you rely on self-reports, or do you count only those people who have an official diagnosis of disability? Do you count people actively looking for work, people registered as unemployed, or all people at working age? Is working age 18 to 65, 16 to 67, or over 18?

Current reports are not standardized, and some very large groups are, conveniently, not included at all in companies' diversity reports. Most US corporations that do make their diversity data public, at best, only relate to gender (men and women) and race: white 60.1 percent of Americans, Hispanic 18.5 percent, Black 13.4 percent, Asian 5.9 percent, and Native Americans 1.3 percent. Nothing on ex-felons—nearly 10 percent of Americans—or people with disabilities.

The point is that unless corporate America becomes DE&I transparent in regard to all underdog groups, including ex-felons and people with disabilities, there will be no accountability. In Chapter 10, I'll get into specifics regarding DE&I transparency—what that should entail and how we can contribute to making DE&I transparency quickly become in vogue.

3. Top-Down Accountability

Companies which issue DE&I reports showing that their DE&I metrics should be improved (for instance, by employing more people with disabilities and placing more Black people and women in senior positions) should be forthcoming in their plans to address their equality discrepancies by publicly detailing actions, timelines, and expected results. And because so many companies regard equality as a core value, accountability for these results should start at the very top.

Corporations inevitably know how to manage processes, to hit targets, and in general make sure things get done. They're highly proficient in building strategies, deriving goals, and delegating responsibilities. They monitor progress via interim reports, allocate resources, add or detract personnel, and so forth. Managers who constantly fail or miss targets entirely are often downgraded or released. When they succeed and hit targets (or come close), they are often highly rewarded (financially).

Given that corporations excel in setting and achieving goals, how do things work when it comes to inclusion targets, specifically in regard to people with disabilities?

Many huge brands are very public about their disability inclusion values and practices. They acknowledge that 15 to 20 percent of the population have a disability, and they publicly laud the value and worth of people with disabilities as customers and as employees in their organizations (as we've seen in the previous chapter).

Thus, it stands to reason that at least 10 percent of their workforce should be made up of people with disabilities, especially because, as we saw, the big brands seem to have all the necessary ingredients to make it so: they wield huge brain power and they should be able to figure out how to make their disability inclusion efforts work. Judging by their copious DE&I rhetoric, it seems that they are highly motivated to succeed at disability inclusion, and financing such an endeavor should be easy in lieu of their huge CSR budgets.

But in reality, very few brands are forthcoming about disability inclusion, and those that are provide only partial statistics, which invariably show a relatively small number of employees with disabilities, certainly less than 10 percent of their workforce and in many cases less than 5 percent.* In so far as hitting managerial targets goes,

---

* In fact, I have encountered only one truly amazing, large corporation that is as fully inclusive to people with disabilities as it is to all employment underdogs, and I'll introduce you to it in Chapter 9.

reaching way less than 50 percent of targets is a complete failure. I wonder how a board of directors would regard a fiscal year in which less than 50 percent of business targets or revenues were met? How many bonuses and dividends would be paid to managers and shareholders in that case?

Top-down accountability means that DE&I goals should be the responsibility of the corporation's senior management and should be treated like any other strategic goal they are tasked with, with similar rewards for success and penalties for failure. But to date, corporate America pays senior managers huge bonuses for their financial success, with no penalties at all for their collective, ongoing inclusion failures.

When it comes to DE&I, corporate America has in effect, *zero* top-down accountability, and consequently, top management has very little actual motivation to invest any managerial effort in becoming fully inclusive. In fact, we not only lack top-down accountability but we also lack any inclusion accountability at all. A current list of CEOs, senior executives, and HR directors that stood down or were fired for their lack of DE&I success could probably fit on a small memo page. Come to think of it, we might not even need the page . . .

THE DOUBLE-EDGED SWORD OF EXCLUSION

Human nature is such that leaving out any group perpetuates the current norm of de facto exclusion by legitimizing the basic act of barring people from the workplace, regardless of their talents and abilities, just because of prejudice toward a group they belong to. And once exclusion toward any group is legitimized, then in time, more and more fringe groups can find themselves sidelined from employment. And if we continue our exclusive ways, we will continue to miss out on some amazing people and talent.

RACHEL'S STORY

Rachel is one of the most amazing and impressive people you could meet. She is a charismatic speaker, highly intelligent, capable, and motivated. We met when she started her first job ever at CY five years ago at the age of 59. As detailed in Chapter 3, CY is a social enterprise founded to serve as proof that a free-market business staffed and managed entirely by employment underdogs can thrive and succeed. Rachel promptly produced the best metrics on her team, and within six months, she started public speaking to various groups visiting or training at the call center.

Rachel is an immigrant. She was homeless for the 40 years prior to arriving at CY, a victim of years of childhood rape and sexual abuse and a 40-year addict with a police record for prostitution. Rachel is at the bottom of the rung in almost every category—an outcast, constantly judged by her circumstances instead of her many unseen merits. The tragedy is that her capabilities are such that after just five minutes of conversation with her, it's clear that she is a remarkably impressive woman. Forty years of her life were wasted because not one employer would grant her those five minutes, and she inevitably remained on the streets.

Once we realize that everybody must be included in the workforce, and I do mean everybody, we need to enable those who have been left out to have a real opportunity to succeed when they are finally let in.

We need to accommodate people who have regular abilities but are less emotionally resilient, particularly people whose abilities are significantly reduced in work environments characterized by high pressure, stress, and cold, uncaring social relationships. We need to eliminate bullying and belittling in the workplace—both on moral grounds, but also because these behaviors negatively affect performance, often rendering those less resilient unable to continue.

For people who are more emotionally resilient, such environments decrease performance as well, but to a lesser degree, and they don't inevitably cause people to leave their jobs. They do, however, manage to make many of us constantly miserable and depressed. We are social animals who thrive when feeling socially accepted and appreciated, and we perform at our best for the long term when we feel safe and wanted.

Feeling safe at our workplaces would rid us all of much unhappiness and misery, and, as we saw in the previous chapter, it would generate financial gains for employers. For the good of us all, workplaces should manage employees' emotional and social work well-being as a primary factor for success.

In fact, I contend that fully catering to employees' emotional needs is such a powerful concept that an organization staffed and managed entirely by employment underdogs, many of whom have never worked before, can perform totally on par with organizations staffed entirely by able-bodied and experienced employees and staff— if their emotional well-being is viewed as paramount. Think I'm exaggerating? I'll prove it.

3

The Incredible Story of How CY Wins with Underdogs

Close to half of 411 companies surveyed had not hired anyone with a disability in the preceding three years.[1]

"They're laughing at you," my wife, Efi, whispered to me somberly as we sat around the table.

She was right.

Five people—all experts in working with people with disabilities—unanimously were dismissing my idea of forming a free-market call-center company staffed and managed entirely by previously unemployed people with severe disabilities.

"People with severe disabilities who have never worked before, have never worked before for a reason," a government official explained. "It's the same reason they were officially granted monthly benefits. They are, well . . . they have severe disabilities," he ended.

The CEO of a foundation dedicated to assisting people with disabilities said my idea was like putting together "a random team of untried and unexperienced Paralympic athletes . . . to compete in the regular Olympics against seasoned professional fully able-bodied athletes."

"Plus," the CEO continued, "you expect them to participate in a variety of competitions in what is known as one of the most contested and cutthroat disciplines in the entire Olympic games—which is exactly what the outsource call-center industry is."

Another expert chimed in:

"It's a really noble idea, but ultimately stupid. You could just donate your savings and save yourselves the anguish," he concluded, while standing up to signal the end of the conversation.

"That went well," Efi said as we got into the car. "You've put five years of thought, interviews, research, and effort into this, and they absolutely hated it. How do you feel?"

"Funny enough, quite good," I replied.

"I know they hated it, but they didn't raise any specific issues or problems," I explained to Efi. "Their overriding concern was finding people who will put in effort and achieve regular productivity. But I really think that motivated people will turn out to be our strength.

"We'll be giving our employees more than an opportunity. We'll be giving people a warm caring environment tailored to their emotional needs, and I know that nearly all of them will appreciate and reciprocate.

"Plus, we are going to be the only one's out there hiring people with disabilities, so I'm hoping we get as much help and support that the government has to offer, and they have lots of various programs for employers."

"Soooo, are we going for it?" I asked Efi.

"We are," she replied, "but I'm really scared."

In hindsight, Efi was right to be scared. I had unknowingly set us on a struggle for survival that would span six years and put us on a supercharged emotional roller coaster. But while I made a lot of mistakes along the way, ultimately we prevailed.

And, most importantly, they prevailed—the people with disabilities who for the first time in their lives successfully held regular free-market jobs. They not only proved that previously unemployed people with severe disabilities could achieve regular productivity and become the core foundation of employees in a profitable company. They also proved that people with severe disabilities deserve to join our workplaces and have the opportunity to become contributing members of our society.

Here's their story.

THE ORIGINS OF CY

We founded CY in early 2008 with the stated mission of building a showcase to prove that all employment underdogs can achieve productivity levels equal to employees at other free-market firms, as long as their needs were met.

I chose the outsource call-center industry because it would put to rest any questions observers might raise regarding employee productivity. Call centers are metric driven, with individual, team, and company metrics easily collected in real time. Everything is measured electronically, like calls per hour and sales per day. As a result, we could easily compare the performance of CY's employees with disabilities with other call-center firms staffed by able-bodied employees.

Because CY was built to serve as a proof of concept regarding the ability of employment underdogs to become an important and integral part of the workplace, we took two additional steps to quiet potential skeptics.

First, we founded CY as a *social business*, as opposed to a foundation or a nonprofit organization—both of which can supplement their revenue with donations.* While donations would be nice, it

---

* CY as a *social business*: The highest salary in the company cannot exceed five times the lowest salary. Dividends cannot exceed 50 percent of profits (to date no dividends have been paid out), employee well-being is paramount to profits (potentially profitable projects that could cause undue employee stress are turned down), and we do not presume to strive for maximum profit.

was important to us to prove that we could compete without special funding.

As a social business, we pay market wages and require market-level productivity. However, our overarching goal is not to maximize profits. Rather, it is to prove the ongoing sustainability of a free-market firm that exclusively uses employment underdogs as the foundation of the business.

Second, in order to prove that real ability can be found among practically all employment underdogs, we chose our first 100 employees and staff from the most unemployed underdog population we could identify: chronically unemployed people with severe disabilities. (Sixteen years later, the unemployment plight of people with severe disabilities remains a worldwide phenomenon, with their continued exclusion from the workplace and society a crime against them and a blight on us all.)

EARLY CHALLENGES

Our first big challenge was to convince various welfare officials that we were genuinely looking to hire people with severe disabilities. They had never heard of such a thing, and it took a good deal of explaining to them before they provided us access to people who potentially might work for CY.

Our next big challenge—after we opened for business, trained our first team, and had our first customer—was getting our productivity to levels that were acceptable to our customer. While the customer understood there would be growing pains, they wanted the team to attain an average of eight calls per hour after three months.

When we ended the first two weeks at two and a half calls per hour and the first month just under four calls per hour, our customer was very concerned. They explained to me that usually new teams finished the first month with seven calls per hour. They feared that it would be impossible for our team to catch up.

I assured them that we would indeed hit eight calls per hour within the remaining time we were allotted, and I even managed to sound confident while saying it. By the end of the second month, we got to an average of six calls per hour. We all became transfixed with call-center metrics, with end-of-day results causing fluctuations between panic and hope.

During the final weeks, our average calls per hour gradually grew. When we hit eight calls for the first time, a huge cheer was heard, followed by loud sighs of relief.

We ended the third month with an average of eight and a half calls per hour.

Success!!!

Our customer was pleased, and we were promptly asked to recruit another team.

We ended our first year of operations with over 50 employees, all with various disabilities: wheelchair bound, legally blind, people with emotional disabilities, amputees, and others. They were happy, proud, and gradually regaining their self-confidence. And even more importantly, they were making friends and creating a social life for themselves after so many years of home isolation.

We felt vindicated. Despite the negative expectations of the experts, things were actually going well. We had spent quite a lot of money on the various accommodations our employees needed, but we knew that at the end of the year, we could fill in various forms and get reimbursed by the government for most of the costs, so we weren't worried.

We should have been.

STEPPING ON BUREAUCRACY'S TOES

As I stated previously, CY was formed to prove that a free-market call-center company staffed entirely by employment underdogs can successfully compete against firms with able-bodied employees. We pay market wages and accept no donations.

However, in making our workplace accessible to people with disabilities, we incurred expenses, such as making the office wheelchair accessible and providing special software for the legally blind. The Israeli government, quite properly, reimburses firms for those expenses that involve providing necessary accommodations for people with disabilities.

Well, not exactly. Or, at least, not for companies like CY.

The problem we faced—but didn't understand at the outset—is that the Israeli laws and regulations on reimbursements for employers of people with disabilities were designed for companies that had only a handful of people with disabilities—not for a company like CY that was fully staffed by people with disabilities.

In retrospect, in dealing with government officials, I worsened the situation by insulting bureaucrats and initiating hostilities.

In one of our first meetings, I met with a high-ranking government official, the head of the department called "Facilitating the Integration of People with Disabilities in the Workplace." (The department is also in charge of reimbursing employers of people with disabilities for their extra costs.) He called our reimbursement request "highly irregular" because they were used to businesses asking for "accommodations reimbursement" for mostly one and a maximum three new employees with disabilities per business.* No one had previously ever hired more than that. They were suspicious because we had asked to be reimbursed for the costs of accommodations for 50 new employees with disabilities.

Additionally, the national annual budget the Department of Facilitating the Integration of People with Disabilities in the Workplace had at its disposal for reimbursing employers on disability

---

* Physical accommodations included such things as ramps and special toilets, and emotional operational accommodations included such things as more managerial time and training or lengthy one-on-one screening.

accommodations was less than $2.5 million. We were in effect asking for a large chunk of the entire national budget, which made them even more suspicious.

Unfortunately, what made them outright upset and hostile was my feedback. I genuinely thought they would be happy to receive feedback regarding the various hurdles employers faced in dealing with some of the unnecessary bureaucracy needed to get government reimbursement, some of which literally flew in the face of common sense.

The most asinine regulation that we encountered involved reimbursement for software for legally blind people. The conversation with the government official went like this:

"We have three legally blind new employees who need expensive software in order to function, but we can't buy it without your approval?"

"Yes, but once we have approved the purchase, you can buy the software, and we will reimburse you for 80 percent of the cost."

"And in order to get your approval, I need to provide documentation that the three employees are legally blind?"

"That's right, and six months of paychecks proving that they indeed work for you."

"I need to provide six months of paychecks *before* I get approval to buy the software?"

"Yes, otherwise we won't approve the purchase, and you won't get reimbursed."

"You guys are asking me to provide six months of paychecks that we've already paid our three blind employees, in order to get approval to buy software for them? Software they can't *start* to work without, that they must have in order to function?" I inquired incredulously.

"Yes," the official replied.

"After which you will approve our request to purchase the necessary software because if we purchase it before we get your official approval, we won't get reimbursed. Yes?"

"Yup, that's right," the official nodded.

"Again, the same software that our employees can't function *without*, can't even *start* to work unless they have, yes?"

"That's right," he answered.

At this point, I lost my cool, and I heard my mouth say:

"I've got to ask, Who's the idiot who came up with . . ." I stopped. But the official looked at me with a frown.

"Er," I tried to correct, ". . . could . . . can . . . what if I provide the proof of employment (the paychecks) only six months after I buy the software, will I get any reimbursement?" I stuttered.

"No."

A month later we got a formal reply. Our request for reimbursement was fully denied—not just the software, all of it. We appealed, but that too was fully denied.

We were in big trouble. If we had to pay for all the accommodations our employees needed, we would never be profitable.

We were well into our second year of operations, we had 70 employees at this point, and already we had to pour a substantial part of our modest family savings into the company to finance the things government hadn't. It wasn't financially sustainable for us beyond one more year, at which point our meager family savings would run out.

But even more importantly, CY had become a home to many of our employees. Many of them talked about work with us as "lifesaving," and they hoped to never go back to the social confinement of their homes. For Efi and I, our personal finances and the continuation of what we had made our life's mission was at stake. For many of our employees, however, their whole newfound life was at stake. It was mid-2009, and the fight for CY's existence had begun.

CY'S FIGHT FOR SURVIVAL: ROUND 1

After our appeal was denied, we tried in vain to get a meeting with the head of the relevant governmental ministry. We realized we were considered insignificant, and we didn't have enough clout to force a meeting.

Then help came from an unexpected source.

"Gil Winch?"

"Speaking."

"Tammy Arad is joining the conversation, and I understand you need a meeting with the head of the ministry, and Tammy wants to attend as well."

I was stunned. I had never met Tammy, but she had heard about our plight and was eager to help us. Tammy was an extremely well known and well liked public figure. She was the widowed wife of an air force pilot (Ron Arad) who had been shot down, captured, held in captivity for many years, and eventually killed by his captors. Her unrelenting and ultimately tragic fight to free her husband had placed her in the public eye for years, and her desperation, charisma, and passion had not only made her extremely popular but also afforded her all the clout we would need.

We got our meeting.

Our bureaucratic antagonist was instructed by the head of the Ministry of Labor (back then it belonged to the Department of Economy) to promptly transfer the relevant funds. We even got a written summary of the official decision signed by the head of the ministry. We were elated. Our long months of anxiety and frustration and sleepless nights had come to an end. Our skirmish with the bureaucracy was finally over.

We were wrong. Days went by and no money was transferred to us.

"There's a problem," we were informed. "The date on your second request is beyond the time limit allotted to resubmit reimbursement requests. You should have sent it in sooner. It's against regulations to pay employers after the specified date. Sorry, try submitting a request next year."

Essentially, our bureaucratic antagonist had successfully tied a knot around us. The regulations cited needed to be changed, but the relevant government committees convened only twice a year—and the ministry's legal department wouldn't permit exceptions. We were getting the runaround by people who had been chastised by their bosses because of us and in front of us.

With the bureaucracy united against us, things were going nowhere.

Our First Demonstration

"We're a social business, right?" I said to Efi one evening. "So, let's do the social thing. Next week the Department of Facilitating the Integration of People with Disabilities in the Workplace—my "favorite" government agency—is having its annual conference. Let's hold a demonstration outside the conference grounds with all our employees."

"We'll need to tell them that we're in serious trouble, and I'm really afraid of stressing them out. I'm really stressed out myself," Efi said.

It was a poignant issue. Until now, we had not burdened our employees with our financial struggles. Many of our employees were dealing with various levels of trauma and anxiety, a third were officially people with emotional disabilities.

Efi was afraid that involving them in what was in effect a doomsday proposition could cause terrible distress.

"I know," I answered, "but I think that it's come to that. We need to resolve this soon, or else they will all find themselves back at home, alone and unemployed. We need them in order to win this fight, and I'm praying they will rise to the occasion."

I had never really organized any kind of protest, let alone a public demonstration with 100 people with severe disabilities. Some were legally blind, some legally deaf. We had amputees, wheelchair-bound people, people who needed walkers, people with emotional disabilities, people with PTSD, people with terminal illness. You can't imagine the logistical nightmare of merely getting them all to the same place at the same time. But demonstrate we did, albeit in a somewhat bizarre fashion.

We couldn't get all the people carrying signs to face in the right direction. We couldn't seem to shout the chants in tandem. We tried marching, but we promptly dropped that idea. And every now and again, some of our employees thought that innocent passersby were the bad guys—so those employees needed to be reined in.

But within an hour, the press got wind of our irregular protest, and we made the evening news. Interviewed on camera, I was angry and blunt regarding our state of affairs. I talked about bureaucratic cruelty, the folly of forgoing the ends (us, disability employment) in order to preserve the means (the bureaucracy, the "carefully" thought out rules and regulations).

I criticized the cynical way that the same office charged with helping employers to employ people with disabilities was callously treating its biggest customer, and that their actions were on the cusp of causing 100 people with disabilities to lose the only job they had ever had. I named our antagonists by name (it turned out that naming them on TV wasn't a popular move with other officials from that and other ministries), and I called for the minister to intervene.

Watching the news that same evening, I felt that at long last we had a voice, that justice and common sense would prevail.

Silly me, I didn't realize that I had pushed a few powerful government officials to unofficially declare all-out war on Efi and me and CY as our business.

Within a few weeks, Efi and I were subject to three separate audits by the Internal Revenue Service and the Israeli Social Security agency. Officials turned up, demanding we give them full access to all our personal finances and that we turn over two of our computers. I literally felt hunted by the full weight of the system. It was scary.

Plus, we still hadn't received any government reimbursement. Time was running out.

Then, a few days later, I got an email by mistake from the government that laid bare their true intentions. Clearly, the sender meant to hit "forward" but instead, hit "reply all." On the email chain, a senior manager wrote this to the department in charge of actually transferring reimbursement funds to employers:

"Write them an angry reply as usual, but don't transfer the money. They are at the end of their funds and will soon go bankrupt."

There you have it. The office that was supposed to support us the most, the one whose interests and goals were seemingly most aligned with ours, was intentionally trying to bankrupt us.

The email didn't scare me. It just made me angry and even more determined. I'd always despised bullies, and I'd had enough of their strong-handed attempts to intimidate us and close us down.

We sued the ministry, and we included the mistaken email as powerful proof that we were on the receiving end of a personal vendetta.

After one or two preliminary hearings and a lot of pressure from the press that fully supported us, the minister himself intervened and instructed the agency to pay us in full. Finally, two years after we submitted our original reimbursement request, we received our first check from the government.

We were jubilant, and our employees were ecstatic with relief. They had persevered and performed really well throughout, despite the stress and tension we were all feeling. We breathed a collective sigh of relief and went back to focusing on our business and our social mission. After more than two years, and not for the first time, we believed our scuffle with bureaucracy was finally over.

Our Darkest Hour

Sadly, the cessation of hostilities didn't last long. A few months later, we submitted our new annual request for reimbursement for our disability-related expenses, on time and exactly as specified, to the letter.

"Let's see them turn down this one," I said to Efi as we sent it off.

A month later an email informed us that the request was fully turned down.

We were in effect back to square one. On the one hand, we knew that there was enough governmental aid for employers of people with disabilities to cover at least some of our extra costs (employers are expected to shoulder up to 25 percent of the costs of their employees' accommodations).* On the other hand, we had come to understand that many of these funds, according to the regulations, were only accessible to nonprofit enterprises—foundations—and were often limited to three new people with disabilities per enterprise. We just couldn't convince the government to make the simple but necessary changes in regulations to allow for-profit enterprises like ours, hiring mainly people with disabilities, to exist.

These were terrible days, and it seemed as if nothing we could do would save the company. Investors we reached out to didn't want to invest in a company that was viable only with governmental funds that it wasn't getting. We had run out of all our savings, and CY was running on financial fumes.

Our life's mission was coming to a shuddering halt. If we couldn't save CY, we would be left brokenhearted emotionally and devastated financially. But much worse, our employees, our extended family, who trusted us to maintain their jobs and their newly discovered happiness would find themselves back at home, isolated and broken. Our plight was confounded by the fact that I needed to start a year of harsh chemotherapy and various other treatments for an aggressive cancer that I had developed. It was our darkest hour, and I spent every waking moment trying to come up with a way out.

And then it hit me. Excited, I sat down with Efi to tell her my idea.

---

* For example, our call center was designed to allow wheelchairs dual carriageway in order to move about freely—without other employees needing to get up every two minutes to let them by. Subsequently, we needed 50 percent more floor space than regular call centers.

"I think I have a plan, a real long shot, but it could save the company and 99 percent of the employees," I informed her.

"That would be absolutely amazing," she said perking up.

"Who are the 1 percent we can't save, and what's the idea?" she inquired.

"The only two people whose jobs, in all probability, I can't save are you and me," I said. "The whole idea is a long shot anyhow, but the chances of us two staying with the company are truly remote. Do you want to hear my idea anyway?" I asked.

With tears welling up in her eyes, my amazing wife breathed deeply and said, "If we can save the employees, yes, please."

"We can't convince government to make the really small changes needed in order to nullify the bureaucratic hurdles they put in our path, right?" I asked.

Efi nodded.

"I just realized who has the power and ability to convince them to actually do so," I said. "The government itself. We just need to motivate them to want to do it."

"How?" Efi asked

"We'll in essence hand them the company and make them publicly responsible for its survival and the employees' welfare. Even though we know they want to shut us down, we'll make a lot of public noise during the process and let government convince government to save and accommodate CY," I finished excited.

"But what do you mean we hand them the company?" Efi asked. "How?"

"We file for bankruptcy," I answered.

It was a doomsday proposition because once we initiated bankruptcy proceedings, we would cease to be the legal owners of the company. CY would be taken from us and would be run by court-appointed trustees—lawyers and experts, who would be tasked with trying to save the company and finding a potential buyer for it.

If successful, the company and all our employees' jobs would be saved, although Efi and I would be left with nothing and our life mission would be at an end. However, if the trustees failed to find a buyer within a year, the company would fold and everything would be lost.

"It's either that or Plan B," I said, after explaining my idea.

"What Plan B?" Efi inquired.

"Exactly," I said. "We don't have one."

ROUND 2

There were 150 people looking at me, and you could hear a pin drop. We had called a companywide meeting to fill in everybody on events and to explain the upcoming changes. I told them everything. I assured them that Efi and I would continue to work at CY during the transition and that everything would work out at the end and they wouldn't lose their jobs.

"Are you sure the company will be saved?" I was asked.

"I believe so and presume so," I answered, doing my best to not freak anybody out.

"And can you promise you and Efi will always be around?" another asked.

"No," I said after a slight hesitation. "I can't promise that, but I promise we'll be around until everything is resolved and maybe, hopefully, after."

"What can we do to get things to be the way they were until now?"

"You guys need to keep on doing your jobs first and foremost," I explained, "and those of you who are up to it, let me know. We're going to make this as noisy and public a fight as possible. I'll try to get as much media attention as I can, and if anyone feels up to giving TV or radio interviews with me, let me know." Quite a few people raised their hands, and then from the back, Natalie raised hers.

NATALIE'S STORY

When I first saw Natalie, I was (inwardly) shocked by her appearance. She probably weighed less than 90 pounds, couldn't make eye contact, and spoke so softly it was difficult at times to understand what she was saying. Natalie was 27 years old, and the last 10 years of her life had been one long ghastly ordeal.

She was raised in an ultrareligious home, and at the age of 17, she snuck out of her house to meet a boy she knew from the neighborhood but to whom she had never spoken (and wasn't allowed to). For an unwed boy and girl to meet and talk face-to-face, unchaperoned, was totally unacceptable in her community. If caught, she faced dire consequences, not only from her parents but from the community itself. But he was good looking, and he came from an important family in the community, and for weeks he had discreetly made eye contact with her when their paths crossed. A teenager, she had been brought up with no internet or television in her house. She was very naïve and had had practically no life experience at all.

Minutes into their meeting, he attacked and raped her, violently, and while he later went on with his life as if nothing had happened, she was immediately banished from her home and expelled from the community. Alone in a world she knew nothing about, she developed a severe eating disorder, was prone to self-mutilation, and spent the next 10 years in and out of psychiatric wards. She had nothing to live for, and more than once during those years, her body was so starved, she was on the brink of dying. She lost her faith in God and in people. Everyone and everything scared her.

When she arrived at CY, care was taken to ensure that her manager and the people sitting next to her were female. We were patient, caring, warm, and friendly, and gradually Natalie started coming back to life.

"Are you sure you're OK with this?" I asked her, and not for the first time. It was a few weeks after the meeting, and we were about to go on live national television. I was afraid that Natalie might be "politely" asked what brought her to CY, or in other words, what her disability was.

She rolled her eyes and smiled nervously.

"Relax," she said, as much to herself as to me. She breathed deeply and said, "I'm ready."

And she was. Under the glare of television lights, Natalie candidly, albeit briefly, spoke of her assault and years of hospitalization. And then she talked about CY, about the spirit of the employees, about the unjust fear of losing her new home that she and all the others had to constantly live with. She was moving and inspiring. She was fragile, but with a newfound inner strength.

I spent most of the interview sitting beside her, fighting back tears of pride and awe at the journey this amazing woman had traveled in her fight for life.

Natalie wasn't the only employee taking an active role in our struggle. We would need an army to win, and it seemed that we surprisingly had one.

Our months of television and radio appearances were bolstered by Udi Segal, a senior news reporter who selflessly adopted our fight as if it were his own and who invested untold hours of his private time confronting politicians and keeping our fight in the news for months. We will always be in his debt.

The payoff came just when we were reaching a crucial point in the struggle. The court-appointed trustees had convinced the court and the ministry of the importance of financially supporting social businesses like CY. The ministry officials were instructed by the court to put together a detailed financial package of available programs for employers and to present it to the trustees and to the court. The trustees would then need to prepare a business plan based on these funds, proving that CY could indeed be financially viable. Such proof was a prerequisite to the final stage of the bankruptcy, in which the court would authorize the trustees to initialize their search for a buyer.

It was crucial during this time to levy as much public pressure as possible on government in order to ensure that they put together a good package that would enable CY (and companies like us in the future) to thrive and that they produced the plan in a reasonable amount of time.

At this point, many of our employees were succumbing to the pressure of our prolonged survival struggles. Some were hospitalized, and quite a few, sadly, had left, as they were no longer able to deal with the constant stress and anxiety our struggles provoked in them.

On the positive side, Udi's efforts to keep us in the news were paying dividends. Largely due to his efforts, we were invited (Efi and I, together with 50 employees) to a parliamentary subcommittee to present our case and hopefully win the subcommittee's support.

CY'S DAY IN PARLIAMENT

We met at the call center at six in the morning, and it took us a full 90 minutes just to get everybody organized and on the bus. Arriving at the entrance gates, a security guard got on the bus and instructed everyone to get off for a security inspection. I explained that it took us 90 minutes to get everyone on and that we would block the entrance for a good three hours if they insisted on doing things the usual way.

"No problem," he said. "I'll do the security check on the bus."

I was hoping that we would be afforded such considerate and accommodating treatment for the rest of the day. We were.

Specially prepared golf carts helped those in need get to the large conference room that the subcommittee convened in. Various Parliament members approached to shake hands and wish us luck.

Our employees had asked to present our opening remarks. So when the proceedings started, I turned to Joseph, who struggled to his feet and nervously adjusted the microphone in front of him. Dressed all in black (we had all decided to wear black, the color of mourning), Joseph looked very somber.

JOSEPH'S STORY

Joseph was born with cerebral palsy, and he moves with distinct difficulty. He has a BA in communications, and he is smart and eloquent when feeling secure. When stressed, however, he stutters, speaks slowly and softly, and loses his train of thought.

Following a childhood of constant ridicule because of his awkward gait, Joseph is timid and insecure. Unfortunately, he has been taken advantage of on occasion. Joseph had been working at CY for three years, and we all know that when he feels secure and has warmed up a bit, he speaks unexpectedly well, eloquently, and with passion. The transition is often surprising because within a minute or two, he raises his gaze from the table to the people he's talking to, his voice gets stronger, and his fervor grows with each sentence. It's as if a totally new person has taken over.

Joseph started speaking while looking down at the table—slowly, softly, and haltingly at first. The various Parliament members and officials listened with kindness, but they were mainly looking at me, waiting for me to speak and for things to "really" get underway. Two minutes in, Joseph was at full bore:

"This company is paving roads many other companies who wish to hire people with disabilities will eventually travel. We should be celebrated, and any and every assistance available should be placed at our disposal. Myself and my friends carry ourselves with pride, and even my limp is less noticeable since I started work at CY. We should be a source of delight to everyone and anyone who has the welfare of the less fortunate at heart."

He commanded their full attention, and when finished, he was awarded a sincere and lengthy round of applause. Many walked over to shake his hand. I believe it was his proudest moment, and I found myself deeply moved on his and our behalf.

Our appearance was a huge success. We received a great deal of media attention and public support.

Several weeks later, government officials finally presented the details of their new scheme to help reimburse companies "like CY."

COMMENCING THE BATTLE TO REBUILD

In the summer of 2014, CY was at last publicly offered to potential buyers. The company had suffered during the bankruptcy process and was generating monthly losses. The trustees' business plan demonstrated that within three years the company could gradually grow and become profitable. But because quite a large initial investment was needed, the court demanded proof of the buyer's financial capacity to weather that journey before it would award any buyer control and ownership.

While a few potential buyers emerged, they lost interest when they understood they couldn't replicate the depth of the bond between the employees that Efi and I had developed and couldn't duplicate our unique operating model.

Once again, time was running out.

The government funds that had sustained the company throughout the process were close to gone, and the trustees were worried that after all their efforts (they had gone way beyond their official duties to save the company), CY would close for lack of a buyer.

"So how do you feel about incurring debt," I asked Efi two weeks before the official deadline for finding a potential buyer—after which the company would close and everyone would lose their job.

"We don't have any personal money left," she said, "and you want us to go into debt? At our age? Besides, who would lend us enough money to put a bid on the company? With what collateral?" she said exasperated.

"We have two weeks. If I can find people to lend us the money at regular interest rates, we can get the company and our dreams back, and everyone will keep their jobs. It's the extreme long shot we talked about before we started this process. It can actually work," I said, unable to keep the excitement from my voice.

"I'm just not sure I have the energy to start over," Efi said. "It's been six years of constantly struggling for survival, and you're proposing to add on a few more years until we can get the company stable and free of the debt you want us to take on. Even if you miraculously find the money, I don't know where I'll find the strength. And you just finished a year of harsh chemotherapy. Where will you get the strength from?" she asked.

"The same place we always do when things seem bleak," I answered. "From our regular source of inspiration, our employees. I know things could work if we just find enough money within the next two weeks to put a bid on the company."

With Efi on board, we put the word out about our plans. We were astonished by the response. It's amazing how many good people are out there!

We were helped by many people, some of whom had never met us. People took it upon themselves to convince others to come to our aid. Some people lent us money they could ill afford to lose. It was wonderful.

The lawyers and businesspeople running CY did everything they could to make our efforts to buy back the company a reality. The lead lawyer, Liza Hadash, donated the full sum of her court-appointed wages, a full year of her work on the case, to bolster our bid. She didn't loan us the money; she gave it to us. We were both blown away by her kindness.

Finally, in July 2014, the court approved our bid. CY was ours again, and a new chapter in our attempt to change the world was initiated.

A NEW BEGINNING

Given all the problems we had had with the government in the past, we committed ourselves to patiently transforming our relationship with government officials to one of cooperation and mutual respect. I realized that my disagreement with regulations and processes had wrongly transformed into disrespect for the officials themselves—and I had been guilty of insulting various individuals. I was determined to make amends on my part regardless of whether it was reciprocated or not.

More importantly, we opened our doors to all employment underdogs—something we had planned to do originally but were held back by our battle with the government. We hired people over the age of 70, minorities, single parents, ex-cons, and even convicts a few months from their parole or end of sentence.

Some inmates called from a public phone in prison, to introduce themselves and ask for an interview. We did not hire people incarcerated for violence, unless their circumstances were exceptional—like the case of an employee whose timidness and fright caused them to commit involuntary manslaughter.

Some people have such difficult backgrounds and horrific life stories that they deserve a second chance. Perhaps none more so than Israel's most notorious female felon: Eti Alon.

ETI ALON'S STORY

Eti was the most infamous female inmate in the country. She had single-handedly embezzled so much money from the bank she had worked for that the bank had to shut down, never to reopen.

However, she had kept none of the money for herself. She had acted fully on behalf of her brother, whose gambling addiction landed him in huge debt to various organized crime mobsters who were threatening to kill him if the debt wasn't repaid. She had acted under intense pressure from her father who had implored her to save his son's life.

Eti grew up in a household and culture in which the father of the family was honored and revered, and she acted accordingly. She was married with three children when convicted, and she had since spent over 14 years in a maximum-security installation. Until the embezzlement, she had been a model mom, wife, and bank employee with zero prior offenses. She had turned to crime solely to save her brother and honor her father.

While searching for a job toward the end of her sentence, she called over 90 different potential employers. None of them would give her a chance. Then she called us.

Eti worked at CY for six months while incarcerated and for another four years after being paroled. She started out as a call-center representative and ended her tenure with us as a manager, in charge of many employees and four different customers.

When a new potential customer refused to have her manage the team that would provide them with service, we explained that we believed that she had paid her debt to society in full and she deserved a chance at building a life for herself. We told the customer that we would stand by Eti—even at the cost of losing their business. They decided to trust her and us, and she never gave them cause to regret it.

Despite her notoriety (reporters repeatedly tried to sneak into the call center to get a photo and interview her), for all of us, she was just Eti. She was loved, appreciated, and trusted; and she was an exemplary and devoted employee and manager. As do all the managers at CY, she made a point of helping and pushing her team to outperform able-bodied teams from other companies. When she decided to move on after four years at CY, everyone, including her customers, were sad to see her go.

Opening our doors to all employee underdogs created a uniquely diverse social scene that was unlike anything I had seen before. Our culture of true equality enabled friendships and relationships to evolve across different religions, belief systems, colors, and sexual preferences—unmarred by bias or prejudice. Our employees—almost all of whom were chronically unemployed and socially isolated before joining CY—at long last had a community where they could thrive, express themselves, and find comfort with others.

Call-center work is emotionally demanding. Customers can be rough, and many surveys from around the globe show that call-center employees are notoriously stressed and unhappy. An independent survey conducted at CY demonstrated the complete opposite. Over 90 percent of employees were very happy, felt appreciated and cared for by their managers, and felt socially accepted and safe.

The average overall engagement score for the entire call center on a 20-item questionnaire (built on a scale of 1 to 5; 1 = very low engagement and 5 = very high engagement) was a staggering 4.5. We actively care for our employees and tend to their work well-being. They nearly all reciprocate by giving everything they have. Indeed, some veteran employees who had performance issues but then markedly improved shared that they practiced at home, every evening, with spouses or adult children.

Has anyone ever heard of veteran call-center reps practicing and improving their skill sets off hours, at home?

When we can afford an official company party every few years, the dance floor is a site so different and inspiring that the venue's waiters constantly cry while serving us. Five couples who met while working at CY have married. At the weddings, most of us shed more tears than the waiters.

We have won various awards. Perhaps the most memorable to me was an award of social excellence from Parliament. A group of 20 CY employees, people who have been totally overlooked for most of their lives, got on stage to collectively accept the award.

Standing there, in the large and packed official Parliament auditorium, they were cheered and applauded by standing ministers, members of Parliament, and dignitaries. Remembering the look on their faces, a mixture of joy and pride mixed with shock and disbelief, still sends chills down my spine whenever I think of it.

Finally, by the end of 2018 we managed to pay back the last of the private loans we had received in order to reopen the company.

FROM CY TO THE WORLD

I contend that it's the responsibility of large corporations to challenge themselves to employ those in the community who are the most difficult to employ.

As the story of CY demonstrates, any corporation willing to undertake the responsibility of hiring employment underdogs will promptly learn that many traditional workplace practices don't work with people who have been outside the job market for years.

Part II of this book is about creating a workplace culture of warmth and human caring and about how to successfully screen, onboard, and manage all employees, including the most challenging of employee underdogs.

It's about how the modern workplace should operate, look, and feel when the emotional needs of all employees are considered to be paramount. It's about the practicalities of enabling true diversity and inclusion and alleviating those currently employed of needless emotional suffering.

I fervently believe that what we accomplished at CY on a shoestring budget can be easily duplicated by the world's largest employers—and most certainly by those companies that proclaim themselves as being inclusive and socially conscious.

There are no more excuses. It's time for action.

PART II

UNDERDOG CHALLENGES AND REMEDIES

4

~~~~~~~~

The Employment Underdogs and the Mystery of Their Unemployment

Unemployed individuals are significantly more likely to experience heightened levels of anxiety, depression, and hopelessness than their employed peers, and these mental health issues often intensify the longer a person is unemployed.[1]

Certain employment underdog groups are globally excluded while others are excluded locally, in some places but not in others. However, both global and local exclusion are surprisingly uniform and actually follow a pattern.

THE PUZZLING GLOBAL PATTERN OF WORKPLACE EXCLUSION

It seems that the groups we exclude fall into two large categories. The first category is *local exclusion*: groups that are partially, not fully excluded, and its members are often disadvantaged in the workplace if they do manage to find work. This group is invariably composed of minorities, people with nonmainstream ethnicity, people with different religious beliefs, different appearances, and so forth. However, this group varies from nation to nation, and you could find yourself partially excluded living in one country but not another—hence, I refer to it as local exclusion.

Muslims in the United States constitute a minority and are often employment underdogs in regard to the opportunities they get, but in Arab nations they make up the mainstream. Blacks in America can suffer from prejudice in the workplace (and practically everywhere else), but in many other nations they make up the mainstream and are free from racism. It seems that regardless of who you are as a person and what your skill set and potential actually are, if you are considered a minority or nonmainstream in your country of residence, then you might have to work harder to find and keep a job than a comparable mainstream person.

The second category is composed of groups that are disadvantaged or even severely misrepresented in the workforce, regardless of borders and boundaries and regardless of where they reside in the world. I refer to this group as suffering from *global exclusion* or *global bias*. Groups from this category suffer from work-related unfairness wherever they are.

For instance, people with disabilities, ex-cons, and ex-felons are severely underrepresented in the workplace globally. Many LGBTQ (lesbian, gay, bisexual, transgender, and questioning) people are employment underdogs everywhere, even in countries in which such biases are illegal. Even women belong to this category, as evidenced by the unfortunate fact that to date, not one country has entirely closed the gender wage gap (some countries, like Luxembourg, seem to be coming close[2]).

To me, this uniform global workplace bias has always been enigmatic, and I could never quite understand how so many different and diverse cultures all managed to develop similar biases toward their local minorities and how they all developed the same bias toward those groups who suffered from global exclusion. It's a big world, and with forgiveness being a big part of many religions, surely some cultures should be more forgiving toward, let's say, criminal offenders, no?

No, apparently not even one.

Surely some cultures or nations totally disregard the relevance of someone's sexual orientation when it comes to the workplace, no?

Flat no. We are still waiting for LGBTQ workplace indifference to become an accepted thing in any country. In all countries, many people from the LGBTQ community still suffer from workplace prejudice; it's just the level of intolerance toward them that varies. Some countries and places have, in general, more culturally based workplace "tolerance," while in other countries, the levels of LGBTQ intolerance are not only totally excluding but, in fact, can also be life threatening.

Along the same lines, surely there must be cultures that don't regard wheelchair-bound people as less capable, seeing that they can, after all, perform and function at work just like everyone else. It's just their legs, right?

Yes, it's just the legs, and yes, they can function like everybody else. And no, not one culture recognizes this fact and hires accordingly.

To me, such global unity in general workplace exclusion is a mystery. Excluding or disregarding potentially valuable employees flies against sound financial reasoning and is damaging to everyone's best interests. Moreover, it's not fact, data, or metric driven in any way. Yet it continues to flourish amid loud cries for social justice. It's detrimental and unfair to so many, and yet globally, we persist.

Was there a memo everyone got that I never saw? I'm asking because bias-based workplace exclusion and prejudice, by and large, seems to be kind of . . . accepted, everywhere, and absurdly, even when the "accepters" hail from the same groups that are disadvantaged. It seems to be a phenomenon with similar deep-rooted precursors across nations.

Understanding these precursors is crucial to any global attempt to further social justice in the workplace. We need to know what's causing and maintaining this global workplace prejudice in order to expunge it. We need to uncover the roots of the real reasons underdogs are globally underrepresented in the workplace.

So, let's search.

Because HR people set hiring standards and have a big influence on individual hiring decisions, we should start with them. I've spoken with literally hundreds of HR people over the years on this topic, and, in general, they almost all contend that they don't exclude any specific populations, marginalized or mainstream, nor do they actively strive to include specific populations. Their job is to find the best candidates for a specific job opening, which in most cases means finding candidates who are a good fit to the organization on two counts: professional and social.

The requirements for a good fit professionally will usually include choosing the person whose employment record and background are the best match with the job's description and requirements and, second, who will probably master the job the quickest. Socially, the requirements are to choose the candidate who will best fit into the corporate culture and whose onboarding will create minimal interpersonal disruptions to managers and the existing team.

In other words, HR people are, in general, looking for candidates who socially and culturally have "like minds" and backgrounds to the existing employees and corporate culture. Which basically explains why both groups of employment underdogs, local and global, are on the bottom of HR hiring lists: Because "on paper," they place low on either the professional or social list of requirements.

There are on average 118 applicants for each job, and only 20 percent are invited for an interview.[3]

The HR objective to find and hire "like-minded" people creates certain tendencies or even preferences while hiring, but it does not explain the global exclusion and inequities that abound today. HR tendencies shed little light on answering questions like why gender wage gaps still exist or why Black women who do work lose close to a million dollars in lifetime wages because of the wage gap. There are additional forces at work, powerful ones, and they reside in the realm of psychology.

THE PSYCHOLOGICAL ANTECEDENTS OF WORKPLACE EXCLUSION: MISCONCEPTIONS AND BIASES

Generally speaking, there are many deeply embedded misconceptions (some of which have grown to mythical status) regarding various employment underdog groups that need to be debunked in order for change to take root. For example, when it comes to people with disabilities who don't work, there are three myths, all of them false:

1. They lack a special physical accommodation that they need.

2. They lack opportunity.

3. If they have had opportunities in the past and don't need a missing physical accommodation, then they must lack the ability to work or are just too lazy, because otherwise, they would work. In other words, most people assume that people with disabilities who can work—do. And those currently out of work—can't because they apparently lack the ability to fit in and succeed.

These misconceptions regarding people with disabilities are global and are the underlying reasons why over 50 percent of people with disabilities worldwide are chronically unemployed.[4] When you consider that people with disabilities make up about 15 percent of the working age population, the world economy is losing a huge chunk of its potential workforce.

The percent of people with disabilities among us has no borders. That 15 percent figure holds true across populations, ethnicity, gender, religion, and countries.[5] In fact, because most people with disabilities have family and friends, the group that's personally affected by their exclusion probably constitutes a considerable chunk of the global population. Working family members of people with disability lose on average six workdays per year to caregiving with the cost in lost productivity to the US economy alone passing $25 billion.[6] Lost productivity of caretakers who cannot work costs the economy significantly more.

Let's examine the face value of the above premise. In the United States, 65 percent of people with disabilities are unemployed.[7] Is that because they lack ability? A couple of hundred years ago when work generally entailed harsh physical labor in fields, mines, or factories, being visually impaired or wheelchair bound could unquestionably keep you from working. But nowadays? After all, what do unemployed people with disabilities do to pass the time at home all day? The answer is a combination of using their phones and computers. What do many jobs entail in the modern workplace? Talking on the phone and using a computer. Well, if they can do it at home, why not at work?

So, with many jobs entailing sitting at a desk, why are the majority of people with walkers or wheelchairs out of work?

Similarly, most legally blind people have some sight left and can deftly operate a computer with the help of special software, and yet most of them are chronically unemployed, as well. It's obviously not their disabilities keeping them out of the job market.

EMPLOYMENT CHALLENGES FOR THE
FORMERLY INCARCERATED

It's not only people with disabilities who are largely excluded. Equally inexplicable is that many ex-cons, many of whom were convicted for minor crimes such as marijuana possession in states that now legalize marijuana, and many of whom worked successfully in a variety of prison jobs, can't seem to get similar jobs when they are paroled.

Again, it's not for lack of ability or motivation in most cases. Even though they have paid their debt to society at large, the modern-day workplace is much less forgiving when it comes to employment. Many workplaces have a de facto unspoken sentiment regarding people who have been in trouble with the law, with HR people and hiring managers willfully ignoring that ex-felons or ex-cons have paid their debt to society in full. The unspoken sentiment is that these people can never again be trusted, they will always lack basic morality, and they're magnets for potential trouble. Therefore, they should be excluded.

As of 2001, 1 of every 3 Black boys born in that year could expect to go to prison in his lifetime, as could 1 of every 6 Latinos—compared to 1 of every 17 white boys.[8]

Just to remind you, ex-felons and ex-cons make up close to 10 percent of the adult US population, a huge group that includes many who have been wrongly accused and sentenced.[9] A 2018 report to the United Nations on racial disparities in the US criminal justice system found that African Americans are more likely than white Americans to be arrested; and once arrested, they are more likely to be convicted; and once convicted, and they are more likely to experience lengthy prison sentences. African-American adults are 5.9 times as likely to be incarcerated than whites, and Hispanics are 3.1 times as likely.[10]

Yet despite the proven prejudice of the US justice system, work-places are not forgiving. To a large degree, employers treat ex-felons as outcasts and their exclusion derails rehabilitation efforts and contributes to a return to crime. It's wrong in every way you want to look at it. It stems from pure prejudice and bias—yet it persists.

The employment efforts of many underdogs are derailed and at times completely thwarted by such ignorant and damaging misconceptions. Despite facts that argue otherwise, these misconceptions persist. And even with the growing outcry for equality and social justice in recent years, and despite all the advantages to inclusion we have previously discussed, there has been very little actual progress on eradicating workplace exclusion anywhere or with any particular group. The only conclusion is that there must be other factors at play.

THE TRIPLE WHAMMY OF UNDERDOG UNEMPLOYMENT

Employment underdogs are often ignored or dismissed because, by definition, they are perceived as different in some way from mainstream employees (for example, because they are older, in a wheelchair, or visibly anxious). But after interviewing thousands of employment underdogs during the past 14 years, it seems that what links most employment underdogs—the real reasons they are underemployed—are three daunting challenges with which they often struggle in the workplace.

These challenges fly below the radar and mostly go unnoticed or they are disregarded. But they are so effectively hindering and damaging that they must be recognized, understood, and addressed in order for even a small change to take root: (1) poverty and acute life challenges, (2) attendance issues, and (3) the scars of chronic social rejection.

1. Poverty and Acute Life Challenges

Many unemployed underdogs live at or below the poverty line and face a variety of life problems that, in and of themselves, can easily drain one's bandwidth and emotional capacities. And precisely for these reasons, poverty has been found to have a distinct detrimental effect on employee productivity.[11]

Wondering how to pay for medication for a sick child or how to choose between paying rent or buying food are challenges that often render a poverty-stricken person devoid of the necessary energy needed to be fully productive. It drains one's ability to focus for hours on end, and it floods the poverty-stricken employee with feelings of helplessness and hopelessness—not an emotional state conducive to shining at work. Poverty drives many potentially promising employees to their knees while sapping their energy and productivity, thus hindering their careers and promotions and at times even causing their outright dismissal.

Abraham Maslow was a famous psychologist best known for his Hierarchy of Needs, with which most people are familiar. Maslow referred to five categories of basic human needs, stating that humans are motivated to fulfill these needs hierarchically from bottom to top in the following order:

- *Physiological:* Food, water, warmth

- *Safety:* Personal security, employment

- *Belonging and love, social needs:* Being appreciated

- *Esteem needs:* Self-respect and self-confidence

- *Self-actualization:* Fulfillment of your potential as a person

Maslow contended that in order to be motivated to achieve the next, higher level of needs, the previous level's needs must be fulfilled. In other words, people who are starving and unsure where their next meal is coming from focus fully on solving their nutritional needs and do not dwell upon their dating prospects or their social popularity in the neighborhood. Ask yourself and answer in all honesty: How well would I function at work if I were so poor that I was constantly unsure if I'd have somewhere to sleep at night, or I didn't know where my next meal was coming from? How available would my mind be for work issues if during work hours, these were problems that I not only had to dwell on but indeed, had to solve?

When I speak of poverty as a workplace challenge, I don't mean not having enough money to go on holiday or buy nice things. I mean not making a living wage, not having enough money for food and to meet dietary needs for a healthy life.

Poverty-stricken employment underdogs starting a new job face a dramatically harder time than their peers and can allocate far fewer emotional and cognitive resources to their new job than people whose basic physiological needs are not endangered.

When a workplace lacks a culture of caring, the only focus is on the employees' performance level and achievements. Employers generally don't ask why an employee is having trouble concentrating or if the employees' basic physiological needs are unfulfilled. Moreover, many people are embarrassed or ashamed of their financial situation, and they don't divulge details or talk about it—so it's ignored by employers. The employee is judged on performance alone and is often in such cases found lacking and is let go. Perhaps even worse, future attempts to hire from the same group will be met by a bit less enthusiasm from the employer.

For unemployed people with disabilities who often need disability benefits and pensions in order to survive, the emotional effects of poverty on their employment experiences are further exacerbated by what I call the *disability pension paradox.*

To understand this, let's try to briefly understand what qualifying for and maintaining a disability pension actually requires from people with disabilities. The person with disabilities needs to convince social workers, doctors, and committees that their disability is severe enough to render them unable to partially or fully work, which is often a prerequisite of qualifying them for disability benefits and pensions. They need to do so convincingly, more than once, and over a certain period of time.

And because nowadays many jobs can be found that aren't physically demanding, regardless of the nature of their disability, people qualifying for disability benefits may need to demonstrate that they lack the cognitive and emotional abilities crucial for getting and holding down a job. Stuff like the ability to concentrate and focus for hours, the ability to communicate coherently, to learn, make decisions, interact with team members, and basically, being able to function independently while performing various tasks.

They need to be really convincing regarding their inabilities because being left without work or disability benefits is literally a threat to a person with disabilities' individual survival. In fact, in order to succeed, the first people who need to be totally convinced of their lack of ability are the people with disabilities themselves. Otherwise, the well-versed committee members might read through their "act."

In other words, many people with chronic disabilities have a deep-rooted self-identity of lacking any ability whatsoever to succeed in the workplace—regardless of their specific disability. Over the years this self-identity of inability becomes deeply ingrained in their psyche and personality, and it is further reinforced by their chronic unemployment.

If, at some point in their life, they wish to try their hand at holding down a job, they discover right off the bat that their deeply entrenched self-identity of inability is the exact antithesis of the skills and qualities needed to succeed at gaining and maintaining a job. After all, they need to convince employers that they can focus, solve problems, interact, and act independently, that they actually have abilities, after years of believing and convincing themselves and others that they have none.

Such drastic changes in self-identity seldom occur overnight and at times don't occur at all. It's as if every month of disability pensions is equivalent to a month of intense training in how to never get and keep a job. Hence, it's a Catch-22, and I call it the "disability pension paradox." Disability pensions are needed for survival, but people with disabilities must prove their inability to social workers and committees in order to qualify, while getting a job requires them to prove the exact opposite to potential employers.[12]

2. Attendance Issues

Poverty can have a significant negative effect on attendance. Research has found that the more financial stress employees have, the higher their work absenteeism. In fact, the role of poverty in worker absenteeism is so important that some researchers believe that financial wellness is actually a key factor in understanding worker absenteeism in general.[13] Indeed, in my experience, many employment underdogs have various and unique attendance problems that hinder their chances of even getting employment, let alone maintaining it.

Personal illness and family issues are often cited as the primary reason for unplanned absences from work. A Canadian study found that on average, each full-time (mainstream) employee lost 9.3 days in 2011 for personal reasons, usually due to health-related personal or family demands.[14] However, for underdogs, unplanned absences are higher because many of them live in communities where the socioeconomic status is lower than average, which research shows has a direct detrimental effect on one's health.

Health inequalities are usually measured in terms of increased mortality (death), morbidity (illness), and the availability of healthcare. The World Health Organization's *Health Equity Status Report* indicates that 90 percent of health inequalities can be explained by financial insecurity, poor quality housing, unstable neighborhood environment, social exclusion, lack of decent work, and poor working conditions.[15]

Similarly, a recent study in the United States showed not only that there are large health inequities between those at the top and those at the bottom of the socioeconomic distribution but also that the gaps have been growing.[16]

Attendance is negatively affected when, for example, employees cannot afford a babysitter so they must stay home with sick children. Poor access to healthcare, which is much more likely among employment underdogs, affects how long employees who are sick or must care for sick loved ones will need to stay home and away from work.

Every so often, CY employees will turn up late and drenched from the rain because they couldn't afford public transportation and had to walk an hour or two to get to work (we make sure it doesn't happen to the same employee twice). The combination of the amazing motivation and commitment displayed by the drenched employees, coupled with their total lack of expectation of receiving any kind of help from their employer (so they don't even ask for help) always make it heart-wrenching for us when we see it.

In general, poor people often have more attendance issues than others, and at times, these issues can cost them their jobs. For people with disabilities, these attendance issues are even more pronounced, largely because often, their attendance is contingent on factors completely out of their control, like the weather, daylight hours, roadworks, or their medication or medical condition's constraints. A few examples to illustrate.

Weather

People need two hands to use a walker, so they can't hold an umbrella when it rains and often cannot travel without getting soaked. Unless their workplace can be reached by public transportation without their being exposed to the elements, they won't be able to get to work without getting totally drenched.

And because people with walkers are usually not especially speedy, even a few feet of exposure in bad weather, between public transportation and the building entrance, are enough to make the journey to work impractical for them. Imagine working in Buffalo or Rochester, New York, in such circumstances—the two cities each average 167 wet days a year.

Daylight

Some people with PTSD are very apprehensive about being out in the dusk and dark. Similarly, some visually impaired people lose what little sight they have when it becomes dark outside. Consequently, when the days get shorter—so does the length of their shifts. Add the fact that many people have a public transportation commute of an hour or two between home and work, a shorter day cuts down even more on the amount of time they can spend at work before needing to leave.

Roadworks

When a sidewalk is being dug up, people in wheelchairs might find themselves with no access to public transportation. Many cities create temporary, uneven, labyrinth-style sidewalks while buildings undergo renovations, and those sidewalks are often inaccessible to people in wheelchairs, especially the motor-powered ones that are extremely heavy and cumbersome.

Medical Conditions

In 2016, 500,000 people in the United States received dialysis. The standard for dialysis treatment is three times a week. Treatment takes several hours, and it leaves patients very tired afterward, so they can't work that day. So, it follows that people on dialysis can work only two days a week. Plus, dialysis schedules can be variable so it might not be the same days each week.

Some people with Crohn's disease take medication that renders them unable to wake up early, and the same goes for the side effects of some of the psychiatric medications. Try as they will, they often can't make it in before 10 a.m. People with multiple sclerosis have good days and bad. Often, they know only in the morning if they can make it to work that day or not, making their work attendance erratic and unpredictable.

How many employers are willing to make amends and take such attendance issues in stride? This state of affairs creates an impossible "damned if you do and damned if you don't" proposition for people with disabilities. If they mention their attendance issues during screening, they will not get the job in most cases. If they don't, they find that they can't maintain the job's required hours, and they are let go.

The Domino Effect

Attendance issues are far more than scheduling complications. They have cascading effects that present an even bigger spate of managerial challenges. People who work part-time accumulate only part of the experience and knowledge that people who work full-time do, so they are slower to reach targets, need more assistance from managers, and need other team members to cover for them on time-sensitive tasks. They miss briefings and training and then require one-on-one makeup sessions.

Their inconsistent attendance then leads to their not being considered an integral part of the team because their absence causes the other team members to pick up their unattended workload. Never a popular situation for the new employee, which in turn leads to social isolation and rejection by colleagues and managers. In addition, managers and team members are usually surprised by these attendance problems and unprepared for them. Encountering them for the first time often causes negative feelings to arise toward the "attendance-limited" new employee.

3. Posttraumatic Social Rejection (PTSR)

Among the legacies of the Vietnam War was the introduction of the term *posttraumatic stress disorder* (PTSD) to the *Diagnostic and Statistical Manual for Mental Disorders*, DSM-III, in 1980.[17] Until that time, people with PTSD were often considered malingerers. The invisible scars with which soldiers left the battlefield often went unrecognized, and the accompanying extreme pain and suffering they had to endure was left untreated. PTSD is assumed to result from a life-threatening event and is characterized by symptoms associated with anxiety and depression such as easily triggered fight-or-flight responses to stress, dependency, helplessness, and problems with concentration, memory, and other executive functions.

Lately, some researchers have argued that trauma can occur *without* a distinct life-threatening event, calling it *insidious trauma*.[18] Insidious trauma, they argue, can originate from years of ongoing, institutionalized oppression, poverty, or from ongoing social oppression wrought, for example, by racism, homophobia, or social rejection.[19] These social traumas are considered "obstinate," and they are difficult to overcome because the victims have had long periods of exposure to the trauma-inducing rejection or oppression, and consequently, like classical PTSD, the trauma has become extremely embedded and runs deep.

The characteristics of insidious trauma are similar to classical PTSD and are also associated with anxiety and depression. But the social characteristics of this trauma carry additional, distinct attributes. Victims are blind to the "wrongness" of their oppression or social rejection. They view their circumstance as a natural and normal state of affairs. The most common reactions are shame, guilt, melancholia, and a self-restricting minimalization of exposure to life experiences.

After years of social rejection, marginalization, poverty, or prejudice, many employee underdogs suffer from and display various levels of symptoms reminiscent of classical PTSD along with the distinct behaviors associated with social rejection and trauma. That is why I choose to call this cluster of symptoms and instigators *posttraumatic social rejection* (PTSR).

Is social rejection such a terrible experience it can actually induce debilitating trauma? It's completely understandable why experiencing a life-threatening event can be traumatic, but most of us have experienced rejection of one kind or another during our lives, and yet we live trauma free. Is rejection that painful and damaging?

Rejection Research

Well, it turns out, that even a small and short-lived rejection can cause not only strong emotional pain but also cause significant drops in our capacity to function well. In fact, research has demonstrated that the pain of rejection can be as bad as severe physical pain, and it can linger much longer. The psychological research on rejection sheds a lot of light on the emotional challenges many marginalized and overlooked people need to overcome in order to succeed in the workplace.

In order to study the effects of rejection in the lab, subjects must be made to genuinely feel rejected. Feelings of rejection are elicited by either virtual or face-to-face rejection scenarios. To create virtual rejections, subjects are asked to perform a task or play a game online, and they are rejected after a few minutes by other online "participants" (in reality, it's actually the program rejecting them).

The most popular face-to-face rejection paradigm was invented in 1983 by Kipling D. Williams while he was walking his dog in a park. A Frisbee landed next to him (hit him on the head actually), and his return toss turned into a three-sided pass-the-Frisbee game that was cut short after a minute, when abruptly, the two others started passing the Frisbee between themselves without a second glance at Williams. Williams's initial angst over their rejection of him sparked the idea.

He created the "tennis ball rejection paradigm," where subjects sit in a waiting room with two other people (confederates) with a tennis ball on the table. The confederates initiate a pass-the-ball game between the three but quickly stop passing the tennis ball to the subject and just pass it between each other.[20] That's it. Two people whom the subjects had never met before stopped passing the subjects a tennis ball in a waiting room. That's the full extent of the rejection the subjects were made to experience. Surprisingly, the emotional pain those few minutes created were substantial indeed, and it caused quite a few negative emotional and cognitive effects.

The Negative Effects of Rejection

Ostracism by even just a computer for only a few minutes was sufficient to lower self-reported levels of belonging, control, self-esteem, and meaningful existence. The amazing thing was that these results barely changed even when participants were told that there was no real ostracism and that the computer was the "culprit." People still couldn't shake the negative feelings their "not real" rejection elicited. The researchers interpreted the results as strong evidence for a very primitive and automatic adaptive sensitivity to even the slightest hint of social exclusion.[21]

That was just a few minutes of rejection. But when the rejection is real and constant, it can cause severe psychological difficulties such as poor adjustment, low self-esteem, suicidal behavior, and lack of social skills.

Rejection doesn't only cause inner emotional turmoil. In a study focused on the effects of rejection on aggression, aggression was measured by the amount of hot sauce participants allocated to a stranger, knowing the stranger did not like hot foods but would have to consume the entire sample.[22] One group of participants allocated more than four times as much hot sauce as any other group—that's right, it was the group of ostracized participants (without control).

The adverse effects of rejection can actually mimic physical pain. A functional magnetic resonance imaging (fMRI) study of social exclusion found that the emotional pain of rejection mimics physical pain so well that it can actually be alleviated by pain medication.[23]

LET'S STOP BLAMING THE POOR AND START SYMPATHIZING INSTEAD

All of this serves to explain why some employee underdogs have been emotionally traumatized by their years of marginalization and poverty. For many nonmainstream and disadvantaged people, life is a struggle, not only for financial survival but for emotional survival as well.

Widening the conceptualization of trauma to include chronic poverty and severe social rejection has important implications.

First, it enables us to view ensuing behaviors not as individual psychopathology ("this guy is crazy") but as trauma-induced behaviors ("it's our fault she behaves like this").

Second, it enables us to focus on the social-political psychopathological causes—the real roots of the problem—rather than assigning blame or individual psychopathology to the victims. In other words, widening the conceptualization of trauma enables us to understand that it isn't being an underdog in itself that causes the trauma. Rather, it is our treatment and at times ostracizing of nonmainstream people from our communities that creates the real problems.

Third, I will demonstrate how adopting such thinking affects the empathy one might have toward underdogs, facilitating our willingness to invest the resources needed in order for them to succeed, as well as our perception of how deserving they are to be working among us.

Finally, this expanded understanding of trauma can enhance the effectiveness of national policies and programs, as well as employers' inclusion practices, and it could facilitate bringing about a huge change in outcomes regarding the successful longtime employment of those people we otherwise overlook.

To summarize, studies have demonstrated that long-term rejection, marginalization, and poverty have devastating impacts, causing anxiety-related issues like enhanced fight-or-flight responses (an employee might have an outburst or drop everything and go home), phobias, risk aversion, and isolative tendencies. Further, people (underdogs) who have been marginalized over lengthy periods often internalize the cause of their ostracism and come to view their situation as natural and believe they do not deserve better.

Chronic rejection has been found to cause severe psychological difficulties such as poor adjustment, low self-esteem, suicidal behavior, and lack of social skills.[24] And last, the emotional pain of rejection mimics physical pain, is surprisingly potent, and is resilient to reason and logic. Thus, people who suffer from PTSR are likely, for example, to respond to the stress of a job interview with a dramatically impaired presentation, high anxiety, helplessness, and hopelessness.

THE DETRIMENTAL EFFECTS OF PTSR ON FINDING AND MAINTAINING A JOB

Employees suffering from posttraumatic social rejection present unique challenges to their employers and workplaces because traditional methods and systems for screening, training, and onboarding new employees will likely fail and serve only to perpetuate misconceptions and bigotry.

For example, a person suffering from PTSR is likely to respond poorly during the high stress of a screening interview, and when they do respond, they often express aloud some form of self-doubt that an interviewer is likely to interpret as a lack of real motivation to work.

If they make it through screening and begin training, they are likely to be afraid to admit that they didn't understand an instruction and will often have an impulse to give up when they encounter a setback. And once in their roles, they may be slower to reach targets and hesitant to bond with other employees, thereby isolating themselves and marking themselves as "outsiders." Because these kinds of behaviors are never recognized as symptoms of PTSR (and it is not well enough understood that it is indeed possible to address and overcome these symptoms), they only serve to reinforce the misconception and biased idea that many employment underdogs do not have the ability to perform adequately or do not wish to work at all.

Having enumerated and described the problems underdogs face regarding employment, the following chapters will demonstrate that they are all solvable. Furthermore, they describe the solutions that we developed at CY, starting with the screening process, followed by training, onboarding, and day-to-day management.

5

Screening for Alphas When the Job Requires Betas

*Fifteen percent of job seekers have said
that they would put more effort into a job
if they had a positive hiring experience.*[1]

In our early days at CY, we observed an interesting phenomenon. Applicants would wait for their interviews in the cafeteria where they usually encountered current CY employees on a break. We observed them interacting with existing employees in verbal, intelligent, and engaging ways. We felt encouraged for them and expected them to do well in their interviews.

But as soon as they were in the interview room with their interviewer, many transformed into anxious, nonverbal, and poorly performing candidates. The change in their presentation from the cafeteria to the interview situations was marked and stark. This experience got me to take a step back from how things are traditionally done and to rethink our screening process for entry-level jobs (and other jobs too) and screening processes in general.

I asked myself what do we, as employers, want our screening process to achieve? Well, we want to find employees who will be able to do their job well, feel good about the work they do, and hopefully stay with us for many years.

And if that's the case, I reasoned, we should put less emphasis on who can master the job quickest because if we want people to stay and work successfully for years, it shouldn't really matter if it takes them a bit longer to get to the level we want. The quick ones often get bored too quickly and move on.

Instead, we should look for people who would have the motivation and ability to eventually master their job and, once mastered, would appreciate our company's purpose and culture and who would be content and proud to view their jobs with us as careers. In other words, we wanted to get to know the candidates and have the candidates get to know us a little too. I envisioned a much more mutual matchmaking affair than traditional screening.

TRADITIONAL JOB SCREENING COMPONENTS THAT BACKFIRE

The more I thought about it and the more research I read, the more I realized that the traditional screening processes do very little to further the goal of finding the best candidate-company match. In fact, most components of the traditional screening processes pretty much do the opposite.

The typical cold, detached, and one-sided approach to screening candidates often backfires and serves only to increase candidates' anxiety, obscure their real potential, and even alienates them at times. A few examples:

> *The fog of war:* The itinerary and layout of the screening process is often unknown in advance to the candidates, creating an unsettling "fog of war" that promotes uncertainty and anxiety. Often, the purpose of the interview questions and tests and/or

exercises that candidates are required to take are unclear to them. Creating a fog of war is an effective tactic to employ against an enemy whom we wish to keep confused and uncertain. Is that really how we should be treating potential employees? As enemies to be confounded and confused?

One-sidedness: Candidates know nothing about the people who interview and judge them throughout the process. And at times, candidates don't even have a good understanding of what the job they are applying for actually entails.

Intimidating interrogation vibe: If you've ever been through traditional screening processes and job interviews, you'll remember that they often felt like cold, disparaging, high-pressure interrogations that were unpleasant and pretty much guaranteed to create significant psychological strain and much anxiety to some people.

Unfamiliar situations and content: Often, candidates are required to participate in an exercise that thrusts them into situations with which they are not familiar and do not really understand. For example, a candidate might be asked, "How you would react to an angry customer who is complaining about the product?" When candidates know little about the product and the company's service strategy and have never been in that kind of situation, it's understandable that the question would make them anxious and unsure.

For a situation charged with choosing a partner for a mutually rewarding long-term relationship (between company and employee), the traditional screening process is amazingly nonmutual. In fact, if screening were akin to dating, a situation (at times) also charged with choosing a partner for a mutually rewarding long-term relationship, many corporations would be considered arrogant, selfish, anxiety-evoking assholes and would never get a second date.

THE NEED TO ELIMINATE ANXIETY FROM THE SCREENING PROCESS

Anxiety can make potentially great employees vastly underperform because of its detrimental effects on executive functions (*executive functions* are cognitive abilities such as the ability to focus, solve problems, think clearly, and prioritize), which are needed to pass screening and to later succeed at work.[2]

Core executive functions such as working memory, *response inhibition* (the ability to inhibit basic impulses and to select more appropriate behaviors), and *cognitive flexibility* (the ability to think about different components of a problem in your mind and to shift attention between them) are all negatively affected by stress and anxiety.[3] The more stress and anxiety that screening procedures evoke, the less of the candidates' real capabilities will be evident. In fact, stress and anxiety are so detrimental and disruptive to a successful screening process that they should be viewed as completely antithetical to it, and care should be taken to eliminate them as much as possible.

The Folly of Enhancing Anxiety Instead of Eliminating It

While some entry-level jobs require employees to deal with significant amounts of stress, most do not. Yet despite this fact, entry-level job interviews across industries are typically experienced by candidates as highly stressful. This means what the interviewer is seeing of the candidates is not their potential to do the actual job to which they are applying but rather their ability to present well under conditions of high stress.

In fact, traditional screening processes screen mainly for anxiety management, and they screen very little for the job itself, a fact that North Carolina State University and Microsoft recently discovered.[4] In their research, candidates undergoing the traditional screening process all performed worse than when they were provided an emotionally calmer process. Moreover, while none of the women candidates passed the traditional screening process, every single one of them passed the less anxiety-provoking screening.

It should come as no surprise that 92 percent of adults report having job interview anxiety.[5] Obviously, a large portion of that 92 percent are not anxious by nature, but rather, the anxiety provoked by traditional screening procedures makes even calm people anxious.

There's more. Research shows that the traditional job interview improves the ability to predict job performance by only a measly 8 percent.[6] Think about it. So much time and effort are put into a screening process that is an abysmal failure at predicting success on the job.

It's time for employers to turn their collective backs on a screening philosophy that aims at choosing employees by evaluating them at their most stressed and vulnerable states— especially for most entry-level positions.

Traditional screening's cold and distant interrogation vibe is not only ineffective. It's often ridiculous. A candidate's capacity to function under intense duress might be important for selecting Navy SEALs, but not for identifying workers' capacity to fold T-shirts, file reports, take calls, organize the stockroom, and even to write code.

When it comes to employment underdogs, the stress and anxiety of traditional screening processes is especially detrimental and can totally obscure their abilities.

In a survey we conducted in 2019 among HR representatives of close to a hundred large employers, 81 percent of employers stated that they would happily hire people with disabilities. They said that they had indeed screened many but that none of them managed to pass the screening. I'm sure the traditional screening process is largely to blame.

In fact, the screening process most employers use can absurdly cause people who actually have proven capabilities, people who recruiters know for a fact can do the job well (because they have had long-term recent success at the job itself), to be overlooked and turned down.

ROY'S STORY

Roy had worked at CY for three years, providing outsource phone service to a cellphone company's clients. His productivity, professional knowledge, and service markers were well above average. So, when the same cellphone company opened an in-house call center close to his home, he asked us if it was OK to apply to work directly for them.

Roy had a daily two-hour commute each way to get to CY, and we totally supported his efforts to find work closer to home. Unfortunately, Roy failed to pass the call center's screening (which was mandatory, regardless of prior experience) on two different occasions, for the exact job he had been doing with much metric-proven success for the previous three years.

In other words, three years of metrics-based proven capabilities were completely trumped by his anxiety-based failure in the traditional screening process. Roy's inability to be accepted to their company was such a harsh emotional blow that it was followed by months of severe bedridden depression.

CY'S REVERSE SCREENING PROCESS

At CY we were not looking for diamonds. We were looking for diamonds in the deep rough. We assumed that most of our candidates managed stress poorly, but we also knew stress management was a skill people could develop and improve over time if needed—an assumption that applies to most people seeking entry-level positions.

Therefore, what we needed our screening processes to assess was not the candidates' current abilities but their potential for successfully doing the job for which they were applying. We wanted to build a screening process that could answer the opposite questions traditional screening procedures did. So, we called our reimagined interview protocol the *reverse screening process*, shown below in Table 5.1.

TABLE 5.1 **Traditional Versus Reverse Screening Questions**

Traditional Screening Questions	Reverse Screening Questions
Can the candidate *currently* succeed in this position?	Can the candidate *eventually* succeed in this position?
Can the candidate learn the way we teach and train?	Can we adapt our teaching and training to the needs of the candidate?
Can the candidate function well with our managerial procedures?	What managerial style will maximize the candidate's chance of functioning well?
Can the candidate attain the required productivity within an allotted time frame?	Can the candidate keep improving until they attain the required productivity?

We based the reverse screening process on five main principles: lowering anxiety as much as possible, building exercises based on familiar content and context, uncovering learning capacity and preferences, mutuality, and fun.

1. Lowering Anxiety

Lowering anxiety is akin to cleaning the lens of a camera. The cleaner the lens, the better and sharper the image you see. Accordingly, everything and anything we could think of to lower candidates' anxiety we deemed worthy of doing. And apparently there is much that can be done in this area. A few examples.

Start with a Friendly Chat

In order to see past the scar tissue left by years of social rejection, as well as beyond the stress inherent in the interview situation, interviewers at CY joined candidates in the cafeteria and established a rapport (personal connection) with them before officially starting the interview. Since anxious people are typically most comfortable and verbal when discussing things that they love and are passionate about, we asked all candidates to fill out a brief form about their favorite movies, shows, books, music, and other hobbies. Interviewers then used this information to discuss the candidates' passions, share their own, and connect with them on a personal and nonthreatening level.

Consider Interviewers as Hosts

Our interviewers are chosen not only for their skill but also for their affable nature. Interviewers greet candidates with a smile, offer to make them coffee or tea, give them a little tour of the place, answer questions about themselves, and treat candidates like visitors who might decide to work for us.

Use a Living Room Setting

Our interview rooms are warm and friendly with a living room vibe, comfortable chairs, a small computer station to the side, and a coffee table—which the candidate and interviewer sit around during most of the interview. The usual military-style "inspirational" signs, such as "results not excuses," are absent, while neutral and calming (so I was told) artworks and plants are present.

Allow Guests, Pets, and Do-Overs

People who feel they need their companion, pet, or social worker to feel confidant can bring them into the room with them. However, they are instructed to not participate or help the candidate. Gladly, this request is always respected (pets, however, are not barred from helping!). If candidates feel that they didn't manage to present themselves to their full potential, they are allowed to request and are always granted a partial or full do-over.

2. Familiar Content and Context

In traditional job interviews, skill sets are assessed within the content area of the role. Candidates interviewing for a computer sales job are typically taken through simulations of computer sales in order to assess their persuasion skills.

But for people whose work experience is limited and at times nonexistent, simulations of these kinds are akin to asking someone who has never traveled abroad to simulate a Japanese tea ceremony. There's nothing wrong with using simulations, but to achieve a far more accurate assessment of skill sets and potential, those should be constructed using situations and content that all candidates are sure to be familiar with—homelife.

Therefore, instead of role playing "Persuade me to buy this product" or "Convince me to agree to this deal" scenarios, we base role-playing simulations solely on personal and homelife situations. Indeed, practically every skill required for an entry-level job can be applied to a homelife scenario. A few examples:

Persuasion (needed for sales): The candidates are asked to persuade neighbors in their building to pay an additional maintenance fee for necessary renovations in the lobby.

Handling objections and showing perseverance: The candidates are asked how they would deal with a neighbor who becomes difficult and argumentative.

Attention to detail: We ask candidates to divide the items in a very long grocery list based on a family member's food allergies. I call this simulation "Try not to kill Granny" (who's allergic to peanuts), but only to myself because having the word "kill" in any entry-level screening procedure is really not advised and might even impinge on the calming effect of the artworks and plants.

Tough negotiation skills: We ask the candidates to describe how they would convince teenagers to not look at their phones at all during a family dinner.

3. Uncovering Learning Capacity and Preferences

All employers acknowledge that a learning curve is important, but many traditional screening procedures often fail to evaluate learning capacity. That's a damaging shortcoming because learning capacity tells you how far candidates can go. Instead, the entire process is set up to only evaluate candidates' current ability.

While assessing candidates' starting points is critical, figuring out how far they can eventually go is even more important. So we put a premium on the employees' capacity to learn, grow, and develop. Thus, assessing a candidate's growth potential is a crucial data point for our screening processes.

Growing and developing entails learning, so we developed procedures to assess the candidates' ability to acquire new information and skill sets and to identify the modalities best suited to their learning style (for example, learning by example, learning by doing, learning by understanding underlying principles). We get a glimpse of the candidates' learning capacity and preferences by getting them to the "stuck" point at a given exercise and offering them different "tips" to help them move forward. Examples will help with clarity:

Examples of Role Playing

In the role-playing exercise "Persuade the neighbors to pay an extra maintenance fee," one of the neighbors at some point starts to raise objections. Those objections grow in difficulty until candidates get stuck and don't know how to change the neighbor's mind.

At that point, interviewers will not stop the exercise but rather, offer aid. They might give the candidates a note with a suggestion of what to say (learn by doing) or declare a time-out to discuss with the candidates what they believe the source of the neighbor's objections is (learn by understanding underlying principles).

In a service exercise in which the candidates' guest (an irritating aunt) constantly complains about the poor quality of the coffee the candidates have prepared, the interviewers can suggest the candidates ask the aunt to accompany them to the kitchen to oversee the coffee making process (guided learning), or they can suggest asking the aunt to make her own coffee so they can observe and learn her preferences for the next visit (learn by observing).

4. Enhancing the Concept of Mutuality in the Screening Process

Viewing screening as the practice of mutually choosing partners for a two-sided, long-term relationship necessitates balancing out some one-sided built-in aspects of the process as much as possible. In order to do so, we recommend the following.

Did They Manage to Present Themselves Fully?

We explain to candidates that screening procedures are often stressful and that we have put thought and effort into minimizing candidates' stress and anxiety. But at times, some people finish the process not sure that they managed to present themselves in their best light. So, it's important to us to know if they feel that they indeed performed at their regular level or if they feel that their full potential was hindered somewhat for whatever reason.

Did We Make Them Feel Comfortable Throughout?

Candidates can grade the interviewers and the process on various questions. For example: Did you feel welcomed and comfortable?

Did you enjoy the process? Was anything unclear? And a general question: How are you feeling afterward?

We observed them, and now they get to observe us. If the candidates are worthy of moving forward in the process in the interviewers' eyes, they are encouraged to spend a couple of hours observing the team they would join if both sides are agreeable. This enables them to get a small taste of the job they are considering, as well as a chance to gauge the team's atmosphere and culture. Current team members are encouraged to be friendly in general and frank regarding the candidates' questions.

Did We Explain That the Rejection Is Mutual?

When we deem candidates to be a poor fit for the job, we do our best to explain why we feel it's a wrong match. Much care is taken to phrase things tactfully so that the candidates' feelings and confidence remain intact. If we feel they miss a skill or knowledge that can be acquired, we make sure to emphasize that should they manage to acquire the skill or knowledge in the future, we would be happy to see them again.

When possible, we direct people to courses and programs that could supply the missing ingredient. For example, people who grew up in places where their families didn't have a working computer (very poor people) can lack basic knowledge in operating computers—knowledge that is mandatory for working at a call center.

In such cases, we will provide them with contact information of various local foundations and NGOs that can provide them with the expertise needed pro bono. When we want the candidates but they don't want us, we always politely ask for the reasons they feel we aren't a good fit for them. We also make sure they know that our doors will be open to them in the future if working for us becomes relevant for them.

5. Fun

First impressions are important and so are "first experiences." Correspondingly, the first interaction the candidates have with a potential future employer should be as positive as practically possible.

The swing side is that interviewing all day can cause burnout really quickly. So, an important consideration when building the reverse screening process was that I wanted it to be fun for candidates and interviewers alike. The more fun the process is for all involved, the more likely it is that candidates will have an initial positive experience and that interviewers will stay fresh and wield a genuine smile over time. So, we built our screening protocols to model escape rooms (without the dressing up) with a series of exercises and tasks that culminate in the candidates' ultimate "escape." It's fun.

THE CANDIDATE IS NOT THE ENEMY

The reverse screening process advocates building screening processes specifically tailored to help candidates feel as emotionally comfortable as possible during screening, just as we want them to feel afterward at work. After all, HR departments are constantly striving to create workplace environments that afford employees the best opportunity to flourish and to create a workplace culture that promotes employees' feelings of belonging so that they stay for the long term. I'm proposing to start these efforts at the initial screening stage—rather than after training or onboarding.

The candidates are not the enemy, so let's stop treating them as such. Let's get rid of the absurd fog-of-war screening processes that aren't working for anybody. Let's get rid of the cold interrogation vibe that can actually cause some people emotional harm. Let's treat applicants contemplating joining our company as guests rather than infringing strangers. And let's treat our guests kindly and nicely, you know, like we would like to be treated if we were in their stead.

Once we correct our screening procedures, many underdogs who have previously faltered at the screening stage will be able to join the workforce. But in order for them to survive the initial few months, an additional change in current best practices is necessary.

We need to address something that is too often overlooked in corporate culture—the new employees' social and emotional needs.

The ability of new employees to fit in socially and feel good emotionally has a huge impact on how well they do during training and onboarding and how quickly their performance will get up to par. And there is quite a bit that employers can do to help them and facilitate these processes. We'll address that in the next chapter.

6

How to Stop Neglecting Employees' Social and Emotional Needs While Lowering Attrition

*More than half of US workers are
unhappy in their jobs.*[1]

Mike had wanted to work for a bank since high school.
He had always found banking and money fascinating, and he had a good head for numbers. He was also the kind of person who knows what he wants and works as hard as needed to get it. He finished a BA in economics with flying colors and was weeks away from finishing his MBA and finding a job with a prominent bank.

His self-discipline wasn't only evidenced in his academic endeavors; it carried into the realm of sports as well. Mike was in extremely good physical shape, working out three times a week and often running 10k races and half marathons.

Then, just a few weeks before completing his MBA finals, everything in his life suddenly changed. A car accident severed his spine, leaving him without the use of his legs and consigning him to a wheelchair.

It was a horrible blow to a young ambitious man at the peak of his powers, and Mike mourned for a few months. But then his positive outlook and ambition kicked in. Within a year he had completed his MBA final exams, adopted wheelchair basketball as his new sport, and was dating one of the nurses who had tended to him. All he needed to do was find work in a large bank and his life would be back on course.

It wasn't easy. He was rejected by one bank because he was told it was "too soon after the accident and that he probably wasn't really ready." A recruiter for a different bank pointed out that he "lacked practical experience" (as do most young people who have just finished university). Two other banks turned him down because they "found more suitable candidates."

After four rejections, someone put him in touch with me, and after we met and talked, I found myself getting upset with Mike's rejections. He was such an impressive guy and so deserving of a chance. The next day I called a senior manager I knew who ran a huge branch for a major bank and encouraged her to give Mike a chance. She interviewed him and accepted him on the spot.

Mike called me agog with excitement to say thank you and tell me that he was to start training the next week. It seemed that Mike's struggles to regain the life he wanted were coming to an end.

When he arrived at the training facility, he discovered to his chagrin that the security setup at the entrance had a revolving door that just wasn't wide enough to be accessible to people in a wheelchair. After an hour of various attempts to get through the narrow revolving entrance or find a different way in, it became clear that the entire entrance setup needed to be changed in order to make it accessible to people in wheelchairs. (This was before it was mandatory by law to make buildings and offices accessible.)

The bank decided to proceed with the training for the other new (able-bodied) employees, change the security setup over the next few weeks, and, maybe, invite Mike to the next training course for new employees.

Mike was in total shock. After all he had been through just to get a chance to start working, after he had already been accepted—he was literally left on the threshold. To be physically barred from obtaining his dreams, just as he was on the precipice of achieving them, was a cruel and devastating blow.

Mike's story happened many years ago. Since then, much has been done to improve physical accessibility in many countries in the world. Building codes make sure that new buildings are fully accessible, and various laws and budgets enable a gradual improvement in older offices where possible. When places are physically inaccessible, it's easy to spot and clear to fix.

And yet many employment underdogs who at long last have been accepted to a new job find themselves in similar situations as Mike's, and they are unable to successfully complete their training and onboarding period. But it's not because the facility or work space is *physically* inaccessible. Rather, it's because the onboarding process is *emotionally* inaccessible, causing many employee underdogs to find themselves part of the staggering statistics of early employee attrition.

This chapter will explain why early employee attrition is not only emotionally damaging to the employees who experience painful failure but also why it carries a surprisingly high financial cost to the employer. From there, I'll describe what's wrong with current onboarding procedures and offer suggestions for a better, more inclusive way to onboard new hires.

ONBOARDING IS VERY EMOTIONAL

The onboarding period starts on the employees' first day at work, and it includes their initial training and their first few months on the job.

Starting a new job is a disconcerting time for most people. They need to learn and master a new job at which everyone around them is more proficient. They must build a working rapport with an existing team, learn and connect to that team's culture, start to build personal relationships with team members, learn how to work with a new boss, and attune themselves to the boss's idiosyncratic communication and managerial style.

It's a lot to handle, and it's easy to see why this period in an employee's life cycle can be stressful and demanding and why, at times, things just don't work out. Some employees just decide to quit. Indeed, about 20 percent of new employees choose to leave within 45 days of their starting date.[2]

Unfortunately, the high levels of early employee attrition come at an unavoidable and surprisingly steep price for both employees and employers. Thus, establishing a goal of reducing early employee attrition is important to all.

Perhaps not surprisingly, some employee underdogs tend to be more susceptible than others to some of the pitfalls and challenges new employees need to face and overcome during their onboarding stage.

WHY EARLY EMPLOYEE ATTRITION IS BAD AND COSTLY FOR EVERYONE

For an employee, losing or quitting a new job in the first few months can cause a blow to self-esteem and self-confidence. In some cases, the hurt runs deep and causes lasting scars.

Those scars have a tendency of making the next attempt just a bit harder because we pay a small emotional toll for every unsuccessful attempt. Just as a string of successes can provide a real boost to confidence, failures can eat away at confidence while sapping our energy and optimism. We can lose a touch of faith in our abilities and our self-efficacy.

Of course, the right attitude, a strong support system, and a healthy capacity for perseverance can help people overcome these types of setbacks. Unfortunately, not everyone has these traits, and those that do find at times that they are not always at their disposal, or that they have been eroded due to a constant uphill struggle.

For the employers, replacing an employee is a financial burden equivalent to paying an additional 30 to 60 percent of their annual salary in direct costs. Jobs that typically have higher employee attrition rates (often entry-level positions) entail an even bigger (and little appreciated) financial price because the costs are spread out among different departments and budgets.

Think about it. The acts of writing, designing, and posting job ads; screening and coordinating interviews; and the time and effort involved in training and onboarding—all these and other tasks take many people and many expensive work hours. Add to these the costs of building and maintaining the interview rooms, offices, and training facilities. Then figure in the time invested by the manager and team in coaching the replacement employees, the cost of their wages during training, and the impact of their lost time on the broader business.

These are only the direct costs, the ones that can be placed on a spreadsheet. However, there's also a significant emotional drain on many people involved, the costs of which are difficult to estimate and are seldom figured into the equation. HR and training personnel feel the frustration of having someone in whom they have heavily invested leave, existing team members feel rejected in a sense—then they have to get used to a new team member . . . again.

It's a frustrating, back-to-square-one scenario for everyone involved. It can also cause lasting scars on the people in the company whose spirit has been dampened, draining away any goodwill left toward bringing in people who are "risky" underdogs or not clearly mainstream.

THE CULPRIT: NEGLECTING
NEW EMPLOYEES' FEELINGS

Try to recall instances in which you or people you know left their job. How many have left because they lacked a physical "thing" like good parking, a decent cafeteria, a comfortable chair, or good air-conditioning? In contrast, how many have left for lack of an emotional "thing" like not feeling appreciated or accepted, not feeling respected as a person, or generally feeling unsafe?

If you peek at the many articles and academic papers discussing the main causes of employee attrition, you will find that the biggest (by far) common denominator is that employees quit or lose their jobs because of how they feel. Employees might leave because they feel unengaged, undervalued, unsuccessful, underutilized, bored, socially isolated, or disconnected—but leave they do.

Catering to new employees' emotional needs is not only a sound financial move for organizations, but it will also enable many of the currently unemployed underdogs to have a fighting chance at finding, keeping, and succeeding at their new job. How to do just that during the onboarding stage all comes down to that important thing that many organizations are unfortunately out of touch with: their employees' feelings.

BOOST TRAINING OUTCOMES BY CATERING
TO TRAINEES' EMOTIONAL NEEDS

Sometimes in the corporate world, means and targets get confused. As a result, ineffective means are left in place because they are either a cultural tradition that cannot be questioned or they are, in some way, an important target in themselves and thus cannot be altered.

Traditional screening is one such example that we have discussed, and training programs are another. Most would agree that the purpose of training is to prepare the new employees for their new job, so that they can exit training and perform their new tasks with relative confidence and success.

If the employees leave training not sufficiently prepared, they face the risk of making too many mistakes (at times costly ones); they will need personal managerial attention in order to make up their performance deficit; and they often get disheartened by their lack of success, which causes them to lose confidence and motivation and consequently leave.

Most training programs constantly overlook two dramatic components that have huge outcome repercussions: (1) the training ends at a predetermined date, regardless of the proficiency level of the trainees, and, (2) building the trainees' confidence and sense of mastery in their new skills is totally neglected and not even viewed as a relevant training metric. Even when trainees need to pass a test or assessment process in order to finish training, asking them if they themselves feel ready to start their job is seldom a part of the graduating criteria.

Using a preset date as the graduating criteria for training programs and overlooking the combined professional and emotional confidence level of new employees after the training period is an onboarding tradition we need to relinquish. The idea that a group of diverse people can all reach the same level of proficiency at the same time is ludicrous. It belongs to the realm of wishful thinking at best, and it should no longer be a staple of graduating training programs.

Additionally, the success people enjoy during learning and training is highly influenced by their emotional state. Negative feelings like anxiety, shame, hopelessness, anger, or boredom have been found to have detrimental effects, while positive feelings like enjoyment and pride have positive ones.[3] In general, training programs should be rife with components that boost positive trainee emotions or reduce negative ones, and components that evoke negative emotions need to be replaced or changed. We want to see people finish a training course confident about their newly acquired capabilities and eager to start using them.

Organizations invest much cost, care, and effort into planning and building training facilities with the trainees' physical comfort at the forefront. Often overlooked when designing the training programs is the amount of care and effort that should be invested in putting the trainees' emotional comfort at the forefront.

Adopting such practices will benefit most trainees, but that is particularly true for underdogs who are more likely carrying the scars of rejection. Emotionally sensitive training programs can be the difference between finding a job for the long term and chronic unemployment.

HOW TO MAKE TRAINING EMOTIONALLY FRIENDLY

The following are a few examples of how training programs can be adjusted to be make new hires feel more emotionally comfortable.

Our Mind Is a Muscle That Needs to Warm Up
After Long Periods of Unemployment

It's important to allow new employees, especially those who haven't worked for several years, to acclimatize themselves to working again. Reentering the job market after a substantial period of unemployment is an inherent disadvantage.

It takes time to get used to long hours of concentration. A long hiatus increases self-doubt and insecurities. Training side by side with people who have not missed any work and are in the full swing of things can further erode confidence and lower self-efficacy.

Training Shouldn't End at a Specific Date but, Rather,
Between Two Specific Dates

Allowing for a more diverse learning pace will help everyone. Think about marathons. For some people, a month or two of training is sufficient to get ready to run a marathon; for others, 12 months of intensive training is the minimum needed to be ready. Imagine if everyone were allocated exactly the same training regimen of just, let's say, 4 months. Orthopedists would be inundated with a slew of disheartened marathon washouts who injured themselves attempting to do something their bodies were not yet fully prepared to do.

Most organizations, for some reason, repeat this one-size-fits-all approach to training by assuming that everyone can learn, progress, and complete training at the same time and pace. We cannot. We're all different, so end training when each trainee is ready, not on a predetermined date.

Don't Make Trainees Squirm—Allow for Social Anxiety

Think back to a time when you sat in a classroom and were called upon to answer a question or demonstrate something you weren't prepared for. See if you can remember the dread and anxiety you felt, your cheeks burning while attempting to mumble an excuse, your embarrassment at being publicly called out, and the shame of being found wanting.

Most of us have had that experience in our past with various degrees of mortification. That's what people with social anxiety feel when asked to demonstrate or answer something in public, regardless of their actual know-how or proficiency. Some people shine the minute the spotlight is directed at them, while others dim, shrivel, or freeze. However, both types can make great employees.

Because we wish to boost the trainees' confidence, self-efficacy, and positive experiences during training, people with social anxiety should be allowed to practice without the scrutiny of the class. We encourage trainers to enable people with social anxieties to approach them at the beginning of training, so they can plan together how various exercises during the training course can be conducted with the trainees' emotional needs at the forefront.

Yes, it demands effort. And sometimes an additional trainer who can coach them in a more private setting is required. Nonetheless, it is still much more cost efficient than losing that employee and starting anew with someone different.

According to the National Institute of Mental Health (NIMH), 7 percent of Americans suffer from social anxiety.[4] Not providing this level of consideration to people who have social anxiety in effect causes the exclusion and loss of potentially great employees who happen to be introverts or timid by nature or currently lack feelings of self-efficacy.

Infuse Confidence-Building Exercises

Training for a new job has the magic ability to strip you of all your past accomplishments and seniority while temporarily reducing you to a position in which you are the clueless newbie while trainers and future team members all seem like veteran pros.

It's never a position that's fun to be in for any length of time, but people who have confidence in their basic abilities or have a sound occupational past can put their feelings and temporary lack of proficiency into perspective, and they trust their ability to gain mastery with time. They can take their temporary reduction to a clueless newbie in stride.

People who have less confidence or fewer occupational achievements in their past will often be much less secure in their ability to eventually master the tasks they are being trained for. And that lack of confidence can create a vicious circle, in which their anxiety elevates, which in turn disrupts their learning and performance, which then further reinforces their self-doubt and raises questions regarding their general suitability to the job—all of which weaken their resolve and commitment.

Trainee confidence is an important metric and should be managed and gauged during the training process. So, when designing training programs, make sure to sprinkle in tests and exercises that are built specifically to boost trainee confidence. Additionally, comparing day or week one metrics with their performance days or weeks later will often demonstrate to the trainees how much progress they have actually made. Finally, don't miss out on any and every (authentic) opportunity to praise, and include praise for effort, grit, team spirit, and engagement.

Surprise and Fun Make for Better Learning

I have a theory. Long ago, someone floated the idea that work equates with suffering and fun should be had only at home or on holiday. And for some strange reason, most people I've met have totally bought into that idea.

As a consultant, I've walked into many work spaces in which the countenance of the employees and managers was so severe that they resembled patients in a waiting room for hemorrhoid surgery. Of course, work isn't all fun and games most of the time, but it should be some of the time—and certainly when it can be used to elevate everyone's mood and doesn't detract from the business. And in training, it's actually possible to have lots of fun during the learning process. So go for it!

The facts about fun and work are that the more fun people have while doing a task, the more engaged they will be and the better they shall perform. The same is true regarding learning, which was the subject of my PhD thesis long ago. When including surprise and fun in the learning process, people remembered more and performed significantly better.

The second most watched TED Talk of all time is by James Veitch, and it's titled, "This Is What Happens When You Reply to Spam Email." The content isn't earth shattering, the science behind it nonexistent, but over 60 million people have viewed it because it's fun and funny. The number one TED Talk by the late Sir Ken Robinson (over 70 million views) is important, informative—and also fun and funny. Whenever possible and without detracting from the skills and knowledge needed for the job, try to infuse training programs with games, include interesting and surprising (and of course relevant) information, and aim to make the course as enjoyable as it is instructive to trainees and trainers alike.

AN EMOTIONALLY FRIENDLY
ONBOARDING PROCESS

Imagine getting adopted into a family in which your new siblings didn't choose you and have no idea who you are. They literally know nothing about you. They, however, have been together for a long time and have their own culture, jokes, traditions, and history.

You would probably feel extremely anxious and insecure—an out-of-place stranger joining a close-knit family, which makes for a really rough entry. Well, that's what happens in most job situations. You join a team that knows nothing about you, you know nothing about them, and you're given no time to bond. Most people will have a hard time being "at their best" in such a situation, and most of us would operate well below our best or even regular capacity.

Social Onboarding: As Important
as It Is Overlooked

If they were asked to demonstrate a skill they had just acquired and were unsure about, most people would do much better in front of people who care for them than they would in front of strangers who are experts at the skill— because they would feel less anxious, more supported, and therefore more confident.

When new employees join a veteran team of strangers who are indeed (in comparison) experts at their job, they often feel inadequate about their relatively untried capabilities. These feelings of inadequacy can cause them to feel uncomfortable about asking for help, consequently causing them to make mistakes, thus deepening their feelings of inadequacy.

Others might feel overly anxious, hesitant, and unsure. They compensate by adopting overly dependent behaviors, like constantly asking for guidance or seeking answers to things that they actually know but lack confidence in their ability to understand or perform.

In both cases, the new employees feel they are lacking, which will affect their ability to perform to their full capabilities, which in turn will lower self-confidence, thus hindering performance even more. In order to avoid such ungainly starts to a new job, we cannot wave a magic wand and make the new employees as skilled as the veterans. What we can do is adjust the social reality to one in which the veteran team members are not complete strangers at all but rather, welcoming colleagues who remember that starting out can be challenging and who are happy to help and alleviate any uncomfortable thoughts and feelings the new employees have regarding their learning curve.

Neglected as the issue is in many workplaces, making new employees feel socially accepted and emotionally secure from the get-go should be a priority for companies. It's not only the right thing to do from a humane perspective, it is also the right thing to do from a financial perspective.

The following are a few social onboarding procedures we developed at CY to make new employees feel welcomed and wanted, allowing them to show their real worth quicker. They should be discussed prior to the new employees' joining the team.

Ask Team Members to Share Their Onboarding Experiences

To make team members more empathetic to new hires, ask them to recall their own experiences:

- What place made them feel the most welcome as newcomers? (It could be when joining a new school class, a new job, or a new hobby.)

- What did their teammates or classmates do to make them feel especially welcomed?

- Ask team members to share from their past experience the places and behaviors that made them feel the least welcome as newcomers.

- Ask them to describe how it felt to be the outsider in order to create advance empathy.

- And finally, formulate the ideas and stories they told regarding the positive and negative experiences into a dos-and-don'ts list that can be applied to helping new team members. The dos might include things like a warm smiling welcome, patience with questions, inquiring at the end of the day how things went, offering to show the new employees where stuff can be found, or the best place to park. The don'ts might include things like ignoring the new person, indifference, rolling eyes, muttering, and voicing remarks like "wtf did they teach you in training?" or "God help us with this one."

Make Sure Team Members Understand How Important They Are in Onboarding

In the first few weeks, ask team members to make sure the new employeed don't eat alone or sit alone in communal office areas.

Remind team members that confidence is crucial and that they can help build it by encouraging and reminding the new people that when they started, they weren't as good at that job as they are now. Tell them to praise when warranted.

Remind team members that the more welcome and socially accepted the new employees feel, the quicker they'll improve and reach regular productivity, and the easier the load will be on the rest of the team.

Remind team members that waiting until new team members prove themselves in order to make them feel part of the team is an option. But giving them the benefit of the doubt and making them feel part of the team from the get-go will enable them to prove themselves sooner.

LILLY'S STORY

Lilly arrived at CY as a 59-year-old grandmother who had not worked for many years. She joined a team charged with providing technical service and guidance to customers whose water dispensers had broken down.

Toward the end of the three-week course, the water company informed us she was so behind that they couldn't see how she could continue. Stuff everyone in the classroom understood, she didn't. She was extremely slow operating the relevant software, didn't know how to fix many technical problems herself, let alone instruct customers on the phone on how to fix theirs.

At the same time, Lilly's team members—many of whom had had a rough time starting out themselves—promised that they would support and coach her as much as was needed. In addition, Lilly's team leader recognized her true desire to eventually succeed and was struck by the fact that she didn't let her many initial failures curb her enthusiasm.

Lilly's manager pointed out to the skeptical trainers (who worked for the water company) that Lilly had been out of the job market for a long time and was still acclimatizing to a hectic eight-hour workday. The manager succeeded in getting Lilly a three-week reprieve. Still, Lilly needed to drastically improve or leave.

With the help and support of her team and manager, she managed to scrape above the metric goal she needed in order to stay. Six months later Lilly's productivity and attitude got her chosen as the star employee of the quarter (three months). When announced, her team stood and gave her a long ovation. Since then, people losing confidence following a rough start are sent to chat with Lilly, and they always return with newfound hope in their eyes.

CUSTOMIZING GOALS

Goal setting at work has been the focus of literally thousands of research publications since the 1960s. Overall, the empirical research seems to arrive at the same conclusions time and again.

There are guidelines for establishing targets that create positive emotions and cause employees to achieve the maximum they are capable of with given resources. In simple terms, managers should define clear goals that require effort (even much effort) to achieve but are within employees' capabilities. However, they should always make sure to discuss them with the employees before settling on the goals.

Similarly, there are also clear guidelines regarding which goal setting practices are detrimental to employees' efforts, create negative emotions, and cause employees to achieve less and, at times, much less. Those are top-down goals that are determined solely by a boss or manager, goals that are too challenging and that employees fail to meet most of the time.

These types of goal setting practices cause significant drops in motivation, performance, and overall outcomes. They also produce strong negative emotions in the form of demoralization, disengagement, lower employee self-esteem, and poor work-life balance. In addition, goals that are set too low or setting no goals at all is also detrimental to peak performance.

Don't Cater to the Wrong People's Emotions

Goal setting of any kind has a significant effect on employees' emotions. The trick is to define goals that create positive emotions and that push and motivate employees to give it their all and deliver the best results. So, in order for goal setting to work and give employers the most for their bucks (wages), the goals need to be in accordance with the emotional needs of the people who actually do the work and provide the results.

All too often, goals are set according to the emotional needs of senior management and their financial aspirations, without involving or even considering the emotional needs of the people who actually have to go out every day and fight to achieve them. When mixing up whose emotions to cater to when it comes to goal setting, many organizations ultimately achieve much less than they could.

Goal Setting Should Aim to Improve Confidence

Employment underdogs at times lack the confidence to be motivated by goals that are reachable but tough to achieve. So, in the first few months of their employment, it's ultimately wiser to focus goal setting on boosting confidence and not outcomes (productivity, sales, and so on).

If, for example, setting a lower target (than needed or eventually expected) will build confidence and motivation, then that's the right move. Additionally, breaking down larger goals in order to show that some areas are coming along well even though the larger target has not yet been achieved is also important in order to boost self-confidence. Once self-confidence has improved, goal setting can get back to focusing on improving outcomes.

Don't Pressure or Penalize Support Line Managers

In most organizations, senior managers determine the company's diversity policies, while HR has a large role in choosing who gets hired. But regardless of who was chosen and why, the person in charge of facilitating the new employees' performance and getting them up to par as quickly as possible is their direct manager.

Time and again I have encountered situations in which management is concerned with the company's lack of diversity and encourages HR to find and hire an employee underdog for a certain position or job. However, if the new employee's direct manager isn't supported by senior management, if the direct manager is given targets and expectations that are unrealistic (given the high investment of time they initially need to put in working with the new employee), things can quickly go downhill. Here's an example.

A line manager with a team of 10 employees loses an employee (for any reason), and an employment underdog is brought in as a replacement. As we have previously discussed, some employment underdogs can have moderate or even severe attendance issues. We also discussed that the longer people have been out of work, the more they might struggle when reentering the job market. In this example, both are true, and the manager finds that they need to spend a lot of their time coaching and working with the new employee.

In essence, the new manager has a team of 9 functional employees instead of 10, and 1 employee who is (initially) a bigger drain on the team's resources than they are an asset. All things being equal, the team is going to hover around 90 percent of the team's regular goals and targets until the new employee acclimatizes, regains confidence, and reaches regular productivity. In the meantime, the manager will probably work extra hours to keep losses in productivity to a minimum.

Now at this point two things can happen. Senior management can understand the temporary short-term circumstances, adjust the team and team leader's goals accordingly (so that they keep getting their regular bonuses and perks for hitting targets), and continue to kindly help their new team member to improve.

In reality, that doesn't happen. In fact, many times, it's the complete opposite.

The direct manager is called into "target crises" meetings and is constantly harassed and pressured by senior management to improve the team's results.

"Where would we be if the whole company suddenly did 10 percent less than expected?" they are asked. "Your whole team needs to put in extra effort," they are told.

When attempting to explain the circumstances they are confronting, they are met with various replies in the vein of "suck it up," or maybe they are referred to the big sign on the wall: "Results not excuses."

The final nail in the diversity coffin comes when neither manager nor team members receive their regular bonuses. Any goodwill toward diversity and employment underdogs evaporates, everyone feels angry with the new employee who is blamed for their financial loss, and the new employee becomes socially isolated, miserable, and lacking in help or coaching. Soon after they leave, and everyone breaths a big sigh of relief while vowing to not repeat that (diversity) mistake again.

RONI'S STORY

Roni had worked at CY for six months and, all in all, was doing well. He was 27 years old, but he had never worked before joining CY.

He had spent the past years living at home, doing odd jobs here and there in the neighborhood. He was trans and coming off a long period of emotional upheaval until he arrived at his decision to transition. When he didn't turn up to his shift one morning, his team leader was worried, and she called.

Roni answered, seemed in a good mood, but was perplexed why his manager had called. "I was worried for you because you didn't turn up for your shift today," she told him. "Oh, that's because I'm on holiday today. I'm actually talking to you from the pool!"

When his manager inquired why he didn't report that he wanted to take a few days of paid leave, he fell silent for a few seconds.

"I thought I was allowed to use the holiday time I've accumulated," he said.

"You are, but you're supposed to tell me in advance and get my approval," the team leader explained.

"Wow! I'm so very sorry, but no one mentioned that to me," he replied. And he was right; no one had.

We still are surprised by employees doing something that seemingly (to us) "goes without saying." But people with little to no work experience simply often don't know some of the basic workplace rules that most of us take for granted.

The more clarity and guidelines they receive regarding conduct and expectations, the less anxious they are likely to be and the better they are likely to perform. Make sure your employee orientations provide guidelines for rules of conduct, clear sick leave procedures, holiday notification processes, security, and other relevant procedures in the company.

Include not just the what but also the who (for example, the name and picture of the employee's HR contact) and the where (a map of where their office is located). Every now and then, ask employees who have completed their first few months of work to point out in retrospect if any important information was missing from their orientation.

Boosting new employees' self-confidence and social acceptance makes for happier employees who reach targets quicker and whose attrition rates are much lower. However, no amount of social acceptance or success in training exercises can solve serious acute life events and the problems they create. But unless these are addressed, the severity of these problems can totally derail even the best-intended efforts of all. As we discuss in the next chapter, underdog "cubs" sometimes need assistance when life throws them a curve ball—which is why we created the cub's ultimate protector—the Lioness Forum.

7

The Surprising Power of Managerial Caring and the Lioness Forum: A New and Much-Needed HR Entity

Happy workers are 13 percent more productive.[1]

A workplace culture that promotes feelings of community and regard is often a necessity for underdogs whose social trauma is significant and who need to feel safe and wanted in order to overcome their insecurities and gradually grow to their full potential. But such workplace cultures significantly improve the work well-being for all employees and generate better company performance for employers.

Indeed, recent research in a sample of 20 European countries demonstrated that promoting employees' subjective well-being is not only desirable per se, but it is also conducive to higher productivity and economic performance.[2] So, catering to employees' emotional needs by providing a warm and caring workplace culture and environment is a win-win for employees and employers alike, dually promoting happiness and success.

If happy employees boost a company's bottom line, what are the main ingredients needed to build a workplace culture that facilitates those feelings in employees? Because we are such social animals, the answer is simple—human warmth and caring.

CARING: THE MOST POWERFUL
TERM IN MANAGEMENT

Studies have demonstrated that working in a warm social environment enhances well-being, augments performance, and improves business outcomes.[3]

We shouldn't be surprised by these findings because from the time we were hunter-gatherers, work (the providing of food, shelter, and other basic necessities) was done with other family and tribe members in an atmosphere of caring and nurturing.[4] We literally evolved working alongside people who knew and cared for us, and the need for such caring is ingrained deep in our psyche—it's the natural way of affairs for nearly all humans.

Ask people to choose where they would prefer to work and where they would perform best over the long term (all other things being equal): in a warm and caring work environment or one with cold and distant social relationships. They would rightly consider it a dumb question. Which of the two is more desirable regarding happiness and outcomes really is a no-brainer. When you think about it, it has only been during the last few hundred years or so, since the industrial revolution, that many of us have left our abodes to work for others among nonfamily members. That's a mere fraction of our history as a species.

Really caring for employees as individuals creates a bond of strong mutual trust—and that bond enables you to do so much as a manager. Knowing that you care for employees and have their best interests at heart enables you to push them to constantly improve and to give their all.

The bond of trust enables employees to absorb your feedback as guidance rather than criticism, to dare, to push themselves with less fear of failure and without resentment. They know that such pushing is not motivated solely by their manager's best interests but that it also corresponds to their own need to do well, improve, and feel good about themselves.

Caring enables better communication, leadership, and teamwork. It creates a work vibe similar to the relationship between athletes and their coaches. When coaches present athletes with new challenges, the athletes don't object, try to lower the target, or goof off when the coaches aren't looking. The athletes know that the coaches want them to be their best.

So many managers arrive home dead tired because of the constant struggle to get the team to do things at the pace and level needed. Trying to constantly motivate detached, anxious, bitter, or unhappy employees can empty managers of every last drop of their emotional energy.

On the other hand, managers proficient with the tools of caring and trust seldom need to supplement their employees' lack of motivation with their own energy. Instead, they can spend their time fine-tuning, training, and improving performance. It's the difference between cheering them on and needing to get behind them and constantly push them up the hill.

We want employees and their managers to feel good at work and to build and grow a bond of caring and trust—which is the most important ingredient in a humane workplace culture and a successful company.

This simple truth about caring has many repercussions. How we actually *feel* at work impacts our general happiness and well-being but it also greatly affects our productivity and how well we function at work. We all know this to be true on a personal level, and indeed this contention is widely supported by research.

Positive employee feelings and perceptions make for higher profitability, higher productivity, and lower rates of employee turnover.[5] On the swing side, other studies have demonstrated that alienation and anxiety significantly affect productivity and performance, but for the worse.[6] And yet another study found that actively striving to enhance employees' well-being at work significantly boosts a business's bottom line and productivity.[7]

If employers can make their employees happy and earn more money for their efforts, then the global workplace reality should actually reflect this understanding. Most employers striving for maximum profit should view employees' well-being as an important metric and endeavor to maximize it. And consequently, at least to the degree employers are successful in these efforts, most employees should be happy, engaged, motivated, and productive at their jobs.

Right? Well, not exactly.

Despite all the research, despite what our own preferences teach us regarding how we would like to be treated, despite the presence of so many dots all pointing to the same conclusions, corporate America cannot seem to connect all these dots into the right picture. Regrettably, as I've mentioned before, most employees are not happy or engaged at their jobs. Most do not feel their employers care about them. And as you probably have experienced yourself, employee well-being and happiness, indeed employees' *feelings* in general, are seldom part of organization's business targets and goals.

The sad truth of the modern workplace is that both employers and employees are missing out on a mutual win-win that would greatly benefit them both. Why? Why is something that should be a no-brainer, not happening? Why on earth aren't all these definitive research findings widely acted upon by employers? After all, employers can be relentless when bigger profits can potentially be gained and inexorable in their efforts to gain them. What's so different in this case?

What seems to be the problem that causes a vast majority of employers to disregard research and common sense and in many cases condone or even actually contribute to a workplace culture that has the opposite effect, one that lowers employee happiness and productivity?

WHY DOESN'T SENIOR MANAGEMENT MAKE MANAGERIAL CARING THE NORM?

As we'll see, the ladder of success gradually extracts a subtle psychological toll from its climbers. They invariably undergo gradual and subtle changes to their perceptions and cognitions, as well as their capacity for empathy for those on the lower rungs. These changes affect all climbers in various degrees and are sadly very resilient to change because they have a devilish knack of rendering climbers oblivious to their effects.

The personal toll the ladder of success extracts from its climbers grows the higher they climb, but sadly, the real price of their climb to success is ultimately paid for by their subordinates. I'll explain how this unfortunate psychological dynamic works.

THE PSYCHOLOGICAL JOURNEY TO BECOMING A SENIOR MANAGER

Senior managers often need to perform in tense and hostile environments. Most learned to toughen up, to develop coping mechanisms, to justify their own and others' bad behaviors (the carrot of large bank accounts helps), to enable them to function. I have often witnessed senior managers shouted at, belittled, and harassed by their superior while they stoically sit there and take it. Ask yourself: Would I be willing to be treated often in such a way at work in return for a huge paycheck?

Senior managers are responsible for the company's bottom line and the organization's continued success. If the company fails, everyone loses their job. Consequently, senior managers wield much power, but they also shoulder huge responsibility, and the weight of this responsibility is indeed heavy.

Imagine how you would feel if several times a day you had to make decisions that could have serious implications for your career and the careers of many people around you. The weight of those responsibilities would keep anyone awake at night. The decisions that are made and not made can be the source of endless brooding, second-guessing, and self-questioning.

For many, leadership comes at a steep emotional and personal price—a fact that is often overlooked by those who do not hold such demanding positions. Indeed, as people progress along the managerial ladder, they more and more often need to make tough business decisions that will indeed benefit the company as a whole, but might also have a negative effect on specific individuals by, for instance, making them redundant.

Such decisions often create conflicting thoughts and feelings in senior managers who have to decide between the good of the company and the good of an individual. The managers' job is to put the good of the company first and the good of the individual second. They mustn't falter when visiting such decision junctions—or they risk damaging their own careers.

Responsibility for the company's success can also cause senior managers to pressure and push subordinates to work harder and put in longer hours, with the result of upsetting those employees' work-life balance and facilitating their stress, anxiety, and burnout.

Yet senior managers are just people, most of them good and conscientious, who would rather make their subordinates feel good rather than bad. Giving too much thought regarding how a decision of theirs could cause grief to someone whom they like and care about is emotionally adverse and painful. It could potentially cause them to hesitate or even make a wrong decision—sparing redundant employees, for example, but harming the company.

So how can senior managers reconcile these conflicting pressures? On the one hand, their responsibility is to the many, to prioritize the good of the company. That, in turn, can cause them to pressure and cajole their subordinates to constantly give their all, with little regard to their subordinates' emotional needs and well-being.

On the other hand, they need to maintain their self-identity as good caring people who don't treat others cruelly. Something's got to give, and what gives are their perceptions and cognitions regarding the degree of their subordinates' emotional suffering, alongside their ability to empathize with their subordinates' true feelings.

It works like this: Over time, the managers subconsciously develop defense mechanisms, which are charged with protecting their ego and allowing them to continue to view themselves as good and conscientious people, *and* responsible managers. These defense mechanisms operate by gradually making them less aware and sympathetic to their subordinates' pain (that they themselves caused), thus reducing their own conflicting feelings and maintaining their view of themselves as good and conscientious.

For example, they can view a situation where a subordinate is feeling so harassed, they are literally on the verge of a huge breakdown, as no big deal and as actually beneficial to the subordinate because it will help them to toughen up. The managers gradually assign less severity, unhappiness, and anxiety to people than the situations and behaviors actually merit.

In other words, climbing the ladder of success causes people to gradually develop blinders to the feelings and emotional needs of the people they manage by eroding and gradually degrading their capacity for empathy. Various degrees of blurred vision for the plight of the lower ranked is indeed typical to a large majority of people who command power at their jobs.

In fact, a gradual deterioration of people's ability to feel empathy can also be found among many low-ranking managers who wield only trifling power. But this psychological process invariably becomes more pronounced over time and speeds up the higher the managerial ladder people climb. (Relevant research supporting and proving these contentions will be presented in the following chapter about the misuse of power in the workplace.)

It's easy to understand the process if you think of it this way. Imagine an employee standing in an open elevator on the ground floor, among his peers and coworkers. When the employee becomes a manager, the elevator rises just a bit. Every time the new manager is treated with respect because of his new station and status, the elevator rises just a bit more. With every promotion, every manifestation of managerial power, the elevator rises just a bit more.

The manager's change in elevation is very slow and gradual indeed, practically imperceptible to both manager and subordinates, and indeed neither side is aware of the gradual distancing between manager and subordinates that occurs, no matter how high the elevator rises. However, over time, each gradual rise in elevation adds up, and very slowly the manager's ability to see and hear his subordinates left on the ground floor diminishes.

Thus, an emotion of distress that is obvious when standing near to the person can be misinterpreted as frowning-with-effort from farther away, and from far enough away, it can go unnoticed altogether. The more power people have, the longer they have had it, the higher the open elevator rises, the less they see their subordinates, the less they can empathize with them, and the less they can gauge their true feelings.

And because the elevator is open and rises imperceptibly, most people with power are convinced that they can still see and hear just as well as they could when they started (standing on the ground floor). Woefully, in most cases, those with power are totally unaware of the damage that power has had on their perceptions and treatment of those below them.

Unfortunately, over time, the desensitization process managers go through often causes them to gradually lose their capacity to empathize with the rank and file's need for a positive and supportive work environment. Many senior managers don't (correctly) feel cared for at their jobs themselves or don't feel part of any workplace sense of community.

In fact, many senior managers often feel socially isolated and alone. And yet they seldom let such feelings affect their own performance, and they easily shrug aside the lack of personal regard from bosses and colleagues, ascribing such behaviors to "impersonal" political infighting (another defense mechanism needed to protect our ego and known in psychology as "intellectualization"). Judging from their own personal experience, they ultimately deem investing in a culture of caring while enhancing feelings of community as distracting at best, and they often view such ideas as naïve, overindulgent, costly, and unnecessary pampering.

And now we can understand why cold and detached management persists, despite being detrimental both to employees' emotional health and to businesses' bottom line. The same people who have the power to decide to promote and invest in a culture of human warmth and caring are the ones least likely to make such a decision. They don't need such a culture themselves in order to perform well, they're partially blind to the negative effects of the current cold and indifferent company culture, and they view such an undertaking as distracting from their business goals. So, despite a plethora of research-based evidence, they just don't *feel* it will further their goals.

But whether senior managers "feel" it or not carries zero weight regarding the emotional needs of the majority of employees. As the research proves, as you yourself probably feel, and as nearly anyone you ask will testify, employees are people who want to feel significant, valued, appreciated, and cared for as individuals, and they will invest more if they feel that way. Companies that do want to instill such feelings in their employees—whether motivated by humane considerations, economic considerations, or both—need to make caring an integral part of their company's culture and managerial creed.

In the following pages, I'll describe the principles and practices that we use at CY in our ongoing efforts to nourish a culture of warmth and caring. It starts with using empathy as a kind of social superglue, and developing company values based on the needs of employees, not necessarily the needs of customers or stockholders.

EMPATHY: THE SUPERMAGNET THAT BRINGS PEOPLE TOGETHER

Seeing the world through others' eyes changes your perspective on them and their behavior, and it facilitates caring. For example, if someone literally bumps into you on the street, you'll probably feel a mild burst of anger together with an adrenaline rush preparing you for fight or flight. But if you turn to yell at the person and see they were visually impaired and had a walking stick, something interesting happens—your anger disappears because your empathy to their situation enables you to see their behavior from a different perspective.

The person wasn't being inconsiderate or rude. They literally didn't see us. This empathic insight into their being causes our anger to subside, and we might even feel bad for not having moved out of their way. Empathy is powerful and can work quickly.

Having empathy for people who are different (different ethnicity, different looks, different beliefs, and so on) is not always straightforward because it's not necessarily easy to understand the challenges that being different creates. For that reason, we developed specific training modules to familiarize managers with managing people who are different, in order to give them a glimpse into the lives of the people they will manage and set them up to have empathy for them. Here are a couple of examples.

ISMAIL'S STORY

Ismail is a Samaritan. Many people are familiar with the Parable of the Good Samaritan, and indeed the Samaritans are an ancient ethnoreligious group who believe that theirs is the true religion of the ancient Israelites.

When the Israelites were taken into Babylonian captivity (over 2,500 years ago), the Samaritans remained, preserving their (true) religion, as opposed to Judaism, which is viewed by them as a related but altered religion, brought back by those returning from Babylonian Captivity.

It's estimated that in biblical times, there were over a million Samaritans, but the Romans and Byzantines reduced their population to a fraction of that number. Nowadays, just over 800 Samaritans are left in the world. Geographically, they live in the middle of one of the oldest and most volatile religious conflicts of our times, between the West Bank (the Palestinian Authority) and Israel.

Considering that in human history divergent religious minorities often have been persecuted and killed—or even subjected to full-on genocide—belonging to a tiny group of only 800 people who share religious beliefs different from those of everyone else in the world is scary. If ever a religious group had the right to feel like a minority, the Samaritans certainly do.

When Ismail started working at CY as a sales rep, it was the first time many CY employees had ever met a Samaritan, and immediately potential tensions started to form.

For example, Jews have a lot of holidays, and some, like Tabernacles (*Sukkot* in Hebrew), are a week long. So naturally when getting back to work following that week, things get very hectic as many of our customers want us to make up for lost time.

The Samaritans celebrate Tabernacles exactly when the Jewish version ends, which caused Ismail to prolong his holiday by another week (Samaritan religious holidays run on a different calendar than Jewish holidays). So, just when we had an all-hands-on-deck situation, the new guy disappeared for a full week—exactly when we needed him the most. Needless to say, this is never a popular move, whatever the circumstances.

In order to nip negative sentiment in the bud, we did two things: We educated our relevant managers and staff, teaching them about Samaritan history (a 15-minute presentation), and we asked them to describe how they imagined it would feel to have only 800 people in the world who share their own core beliefs.

By helping our staff understand who the Samaritans are, where they came from, and their minority situation, we helped to create empathy and enabled our employees to develop a different perspective.

I then searched for cool Samaritan traditions in order to create affinity with their religion. I found many.

For example, during Tabernacles, it's a Jewish and Samaritan tradition to build and decorate a small hut. However (and hoping no one takes offense), the difference between the Jewish decorations and those of the Samaritans is dramatic. Most Jews make do with a few colorful paper chains and kiddie-drawn stuff hanging from the ceiling. The Samaritans, on the other hand, invest days, and their results are breathtaking—for instance, covering the entire ceiling of the hut with closely packed fruit, creating a mosaic of colors and patterns.

Showing CY employees pictures of Samaritan Tabernacles huts not only enhanced empathy but also appreciation and acceptance. Plus, lots of people wanted to visit Mount Gerizim to witness the Samaritan Tabernacles with their own eyes.

People understood why Ismail was away, and his perceived motivations changed from shirking work when it got intense to upholding lovely ancient family traditions in a society so small that each person's presence was crucial. Ismail has been at CY for over 11 years and is now a project leader, loved and respected by everyone at CY, adored by his team, as well as the customers his team serves. He is an amazing person and a huge asset.

PAST EXPERIENCES IN THE SERVICE OF EMPATHY

It's really difficult to go through life without some personal experience of being shunned, feeling like an outsider, not being understood, or not being connected. For some, these experiences occurred in their youth while others encountered them later on in life, but by and large, we've all had occasion to feel like an outcast or outsider at some point, and we remember the sting of it well.

We remind people of those occasions, and we discuss the people that made them feel that way, what they did or didn't do to make them feel unwanted, and their dismal feelings at the time. Such sessions are not only powerful ways to create empathy for new employees but they also serve to create scorn for the past perpetrators while enhancing people's aversion to behaving in such a way themselves.

HARVEY'S STORY

Harvey was a high-functioning person with autism spectrum disorder (ASD). His first interview at CY went well. On the day of his second interview, however, things started out badly.

He couldn't get his shoes to feel right on his feet, and trying to adjust one of his socks while drinking his morning coffee caused him to spill coffee on his shirt. The wardrobe change caused him to miss the bus and arrive just before his second interview, but without time to calm himself mentally.

He couldn't shake his irritation, his shoes still felt "wrong," and he had a hard time concentrating on the questions and tasks. The interviewer stopped the interview midway, realizing there was a large discrepancy between the first interviewer's assessment and Harvey's current performance. She asked him if he felt differently from how he felt during his first visit. He did. They decided together to let Harvey go to the cafeteria and relax, fix his shoes (or socks), calm himself, and restart the interview in an hour.

The interviewer later explained the situation to a new team member. "Remember a few weeks ago when you had that lower back pain that was driving you crazy? Remember how cranky you were?"

People with ASD can feel that upset and even more so, just from something minor not working out for them. High volume of upset, much smaller triggers. If we want to assess Harvey's true potential, we need to see him when he's not preoccupied with an irritant.

VALUES: THE PRINCIPLES UNDERLYING CORPORATE CULTURE

Teamwork is one of the most popular company values, at least according to one website, and I have indeed worked with many large organizations that have chosen teamwork as one of their core values.[8]

Not long ago, I asked the CEO of a large company that had defined teamwork as their number one core value about the process by which this specific value was chosen.

"I consulted with a consulting company about a list of values I thought were important and narrowed it down to five values, and I then presented them for approval to our senior managers," he replied.

"You didn't use teamwork to determine your values?" I gently inquired.

"Values are extremely important and shouldn't be determined by people who are not 100 percent in sync with our purpose and strategy," he replied in a huff.

The conversation pretty much sums up the dismal and hypocritical reality of most corporate values I have encountered.

Indeed, over the past 30 years, I've come across very few organizations that really take their values seriously—that is, they make sure all employees actually know what the values are, they encourage employees to uphold them, and senior managers strive to set a personal example and lead from the front.

Apparently, I'm not the only one who thinks that most companies' values are more lip service than ethical and behavioral guidelines. In a survey by Gallup, only 27 percent of employees strongly believed in their organization's core values, and in many cases, employees aren't even sure what their company's values are.[9] Because at CY we take our values seriously indeed, we defined the following four standards we need to uphold in order to fuse our values to the company culture and everyday life.

THE FOUR KEYS TO SUCCESSFULLY UPHOLDING COMPANY VALUES

When a company takes its values seriously, those values are mirrored by the company's culture and they drive behavior, causing managers and employees to actively strive to uphold them. There are four components in making that happen:

1. Managers and employees need to understand the necessity of the value—why it's needed.

2. They also need to know the implications (if any) of not upholding the value—the "if-not" consideration.

3. The value needs to be part of everyday life and discussed often.

4. And lastly, they need to see the value modeled from the top down in order to believe the sincerity of the organization's intentions.

Here's a short illustration, using CY's core value of equality.

I believe that happy and cared for employees are a crucial ingredient for real diversity (otherwise, some employees remain excluded from the company's diversity efforts and culture) and that a happy and diverse workforce is crucial for any company's success.

In order to cultivate a strong corporate culture of caring and employee well-being and happiness, we decided to adopt core values that would promote such behaviors and facilitate strong feelings of community. Correspondingly, CY's most important core value is equality.

All staff and management go through periodic training and discussions in order to help them actively strive to uphold our values. This is how we use the four principles to fuse the value of equality to company culture.

The Why of Equality

We explain why we need the value of equality by providing research findings on the immense negative impact rejection and marginalization can have on people. We discuss the emotional scars they leave and how those past hurts can affect various behaviors in the workplace, such as fight-or flight-responses.

We explain that when people have been looked down on all their lives and they feel as outsiders, of lesser status, the last thing they need is someone talking down to them. Being talked down to will just reinforce their trauma and make their attempts to master their new job less likely to succeed.

We also discuss which behaviors and attitudes toward others can help mend these scars and mitigate the effects of rejection, and which behaviors could deepen them. We teach how to manage employee anger or frustration in a way that respects them and does not escalate the situation, as well as how to recover if managers do step out of line or lose their cool (that is, taking responsibility and apologizing, never ignoring).

The "If Not" of Equality

Values training in CY also addresses what a junior staff member does when witnessing a senior staff member not speaking respectfully to an employee—the "if not."

The junior staff member should approach the out-of-line senior one and stand close to their side for three seconds, touch them on the shoulder, and then leave and never address it again.

The rationale of this is as follows. Standing within a person's personal space and touching their shoulder serves to give the out-of-line manager an opportunity to disengage for a second and realize they are letting their temper get the best of them. Not addressing it again saves them both the dual embarrassment of a senior manager explaining to a subordinate why they "lost it." Plus, it serves to reduce the potency of the whole incident, thus making the whole thing more palatable and likely to become part of the company's culture.

Discussing Equality

It's important to discuss equality. Here's an example from CY. When an employee is chosen as the employee of the month, we hold a public affair with cookies and celebrations.

When we discuss why the person won the award, we stress the number one reason for the selection was how the employee's behaviors and attitudes aligned with the values of the company.

Top Down

As the CEO, I often explain that there are people well below me who are more intelligent than I am, or better citizens, or better people in general. My seniority doesn't make me better than others at all or in any way. It just means that I get to make decisions.

Everyone must be treated with respect regardless of their position in the company, and especially by senior staff. If we truly want the value of equality to trickle down throughout the company and embed itself in our company culture, it has to be constantly modeled and addressed by senior staff and managers.

At CY all our values are aimed at catering to the emotional needs of our employees. The better we take care of them, the more caring and warm our culture, the better our employees take care of our customers and ultimately, our business. Employers who wish to not only employ underdogs but indeed to win with them and get the most out of their motivations and talent, take heed. A culture of caring and warmth is a huge part of creating the environment underdogs need in order to flourish and become the best they can be. It's not overindulgent costly pampering. It's just good business.

Unfortunately, even the nicest and kindest workplace can do little to shield some underdogs from various life problems that originate outside of the workplace. Every now and then, employees find themselves dealing with life issues that affect their ability to perform their jobs well. They get sick and have no one to care for them, they get evicted and have nowhere to stay, they are alone in town and have nowhere to go for the holidays, or they have debt and don't have enough money to buy food for themselves or get to work.

But what if it were possible to solve these challenges in a way that does not take away from a company's bottom line and has the added benefit of increasing employee engagement, esprit de corps, a sense of belonging and motivation, while actually reducing employee attrition and sick days?

ADI'S STORY

Adi was a 45-year-old single man, who lived alone and had no immediate family in the country. When his manager visited him in the hospital following complicated back surgery, he mentioned that in two days he would be discharged home, but he would need two weeks of mandatory bed rest.

"So, who's going to do shopping, prepare your food?" she inquired.

After a few seconds of silence, Adi said quietly, "I don't have anyone."

When Adi's manager realized that, in two days, he would find himself bedridden and alone, she was distraught and at a loss. (At CY the function of the Lioness Forum is performed by one person, but she was on holiday and unavailable.)

She still couldn't shake it the next day and found herself talking about it during her team's morning briefing. And then an amazing thing happened. Her team, all of whom were underdogs, many with their own life problems, spontaneously opened a "situation room" in the cafeteria, and during their breaks, got to work, as if they had decided to unofficially create their own Lioness Forum. They were quickly joined by other employees and managers.

The Lioness Forum found a restaurant that was willing to provide three meals a day for two weeks. They located a taxi company that operated adjacent to the restaurant, that was willing to deliver the meals to Adi. Employees that lived in proximity to Adi set up their shifts so that they could help with meals three times a day. And finally, three male employees took turns helping Adi make it to the shower and bathroom and back.

The effect of this team effort swept the entire company, raising team spirit and enhancing the sense of camaraderie and belonging. Even more than before, employees felt like part of a family, a community that would look out for them in times of need. It created a deeper sense of security, and it even effected employees' efficacy. It made our chain stronger.

THE LIONESS FORUM: A NEW HR ENTITY

Many companies have employee assistance programs (EAPs), which is a great thing—in theory. However, a recent (2020) poll taken by the American Psychiatric Association showed that about half of American workers are concerned about discussing mental health issues in the workplace, and a third worry about consequences if they seek help through official work channels.[10]

It's not surprising, then, that workers are apprehensive about discussing personal issues and problems with workplace officials and managers, especially if those problems hinder their performance and might be used to justify their dismissal. Of course, their apprehension about disclosing their issues doesn't make the problems go away or stop their detrimental effects on job performance.

Our solution at CY was to create a novel entity, one that made employees feel protected (much like lion cubs feel protected by the lioness—hence the name "Lioness" or "Lioness Forum").

The Lioness Forum is a non-HR entity composed of veteran, kindhearted, and proactive employees who assist other employees with acute life challenges by finding people in the community who can help. Helpers from the community might include, for example, a lawyer who will offer pro bono help with a foreclosure on an employee's bank account; a hotel that can put up the battered wife and kids for a few nights; or an accountant who will help an employee navigate the bureaucracy needed to place their newly diagnosed kid in a school that specializes in kids on the spectrum.

The Lioness Forum at CY

At CY, the function of the Lioness Forum is performed by one person. She is charged with taking care of employees' life problems that have no direct connection to the workplace but negatively affect the ability of employees to succeed and concentrate at work. She operates with no financial resources at her disposal!

Her tools are kindness and caring, patience, and unrelentless persistence on behalf of her "cubs." The lioness knows that the world is full of good and kind people, and she has a knack of recruiting them, pro bono, in the aid of our employees.

Because many companies have, every now and again, employees facing life problems that they cannot handle on their own, I strongly advocate creating a company Lioness Forum. Because of the demanding complexity of the job, I recommend that the Lioness Forum consist of three people who not only provide emotional support and assistance to company employees who need help that is beyond the scope of regular HR departments but also attempt to assist in solving employees' life problems.

And just like the lioness, their tools should be kindness, caring, ingenuity, and persistence with no financial resources (the company's or their own). In brief, this is how I recommend companies go about creating their own Lioness Forum.

DIANA'S STORY

For one fleeting second, it was Diana's happiest moment ever. Diana was a single mom, and her daughter had just told her that she would be marrying her boyfriend of two years and that his folks would be paying for most of the wedding.

Diana was overjoyed with her daughter's happiness, and because she was very poor, she was especially happy that her in-laws were better off financially and thrilled that they were prepared to pay for most of the wedding.

And then the difference between all and most dawned on her, and her happiness evaporated, displaced by dread. She had no savings at all. She couldn't afford to pay for a nice dress, let alone for "some" of the wedding.

She put on a smile for her daughter, but she became totally preoccupied with financing her part of the wedding. Her preoccupation didn't dissipate at work. At the end of her shift, she made a beeline for the lioness's office.

The lioness never gives people money. Rather, she gets pro bono professional aid when needed (lawyers, accountants, dentists) or "things" like a hotel room, a fridge, or food. But in this case, money was needed. Deciding to forgo her no-money rule in this case, she swore Diana to secrecy and then sat down to start writing emails. Within a week, she had managed to collect enough to pay for Diana's (very modest) part of the wedding costs and for a nice new dress and shoes for Diana to wear to the event.

The Who and How of Creating a Lioness Forum

How to choose the right people, maintain anonymity, and conduct operations.

Who

Many people feel at some point in their life that they have a need to give, and they look for places or people in the community to whom they might be able to be of assistance. Companies will be surprised at how many of their employees will be honored to volunteer their time and effort for the Lioness Forum.

The Lioness Forum should consist of about three willing and eager veteran employees and managers from the company's rank and file.

How

These are the important aspects to focus on:

- *Forum members:* Create organizational buzz to recruit candidates throughout the organization. Perhaps the same people responsible for the company's public relations should put together the "employee relations" campaign. The campaign should detail the "job description," which should emphasize the need for people who are kind, caring, capable, discreet, and motivated to help others. Direct managers submit applicants to HR.

- *Anonymity:* Forum members sign a document stating they are not allowed to divulge to any other employees any information regarding a candidate's identity and the nature of aid needed. Applicants in need of the forum send an anonymous request to the forum's inbox. Each request should be designated by a number. The forum periodically announces which numbers (cases) are accepted, and only then do they meet the applicant (employee in need). They don't know the identity of the employees whose cases they didn't accept (for example, an employee with consistent gambling debts). The forum operates independently from HR, and HR does not know who approached and who is being helped.

- *Legal aspects:* Candidates sign a disclaimer that the company has no legal obligation or responsibility regarding the help the forum offers (you should consult with legal when wording the disclaimer, but keep it simple). The forum is voluntary both ways—candidates choose to apply, and forum members volunteer their help.

- *Administration:* HR is in charge of choosing the forum members and all administration aspects, such as coordination of meetings and the venue. However, HR never participates in the forum meetings.

- *Meetings:* The forum meets weekly when taking care of a case, before or after official work hours. In between meetings, members operate on their own free time and report back to the group digitally. The group is headed and meetings are led by the group leader who is chosen by HR (according to suitability, not rank or seniority).

- *Management involvement:* The Lioness Forum should be heralded by management, and once or twice a year should hold meetings outside the office, on company time and in a venue paid for by the company. The venue should be cool, fun, or posh.

- *Length of service:* Service on the Lioness Forum should be limited to two years, to avoid the forum's becoming any single person's show.

ZOE'S STORY

Zoe wasn't herself. For the past couple of days she had seemed detached and forlorn. When called in to chat with her manager, she shared that she had just broken up with her boyfriend of many years, and he took all their pictures with him when he left.

Because Zoe is legally blind and gradually losing the little that's left of her eyesight, she was overcome with fear that without any recent pictures of herself to look at, she might, over time, entirely forget her appearance. The manager sent Zoe to speak to the lioness. Within a week, the lioness had put together a pro bono team of a hair stylist, makeup artist, and photographer. A few days later, Zoe was seen sitting in the cafeteria, engraving in her memory what she looks like while intently staring at the beautiful pictures of herself in her new photographic album.

THE LIONESS MOTTO

Creating a company culture that cultivates feelings of community and caring can be achieved by using empathy and company core values and by establishing and maintaining a Lioness Forum. Such a culture will improve employees' sense of community, belonging, and general well-being—which in turn will significantly increase employee engagement and productivity and subsequently will significantly and positively affect the company's bottom line.

> Lioness Forum Motto: HR's job is to care for you
> as an employee, and ours is to care for you as
> a member of our family and community.

Efforts to create a caring workplace often face a common nemesis because the most disruptive force to a warm and supportive work culture is an instance of misused managerial power.

Having power over people who are insecure, marginalized, have faced injustice, and feel left out makes that power even more potent and its misuse even more damaging. Nothing can shatter an employee's feelings of security and caring like being witness or falling victim to workplace bullying

The misuse of managerial power, at all levels, must be addressed and guarded against in all workplaces. Unfortunately, the following chapter will demonstrate that despite the widespread damage that workplace harassment, bullying, and managerial power abuses inflict, they are often ignored.

Acknowledging and Eradicating Workplace Bullying and Power Abuse

O, it is excellent
To have a giant's strength, but it is tyrannous
To use it like a giant.

—William Shakespeare,
Measure for Measure, Act 2, Scene 2

"

We wanted to consult with you regarding problems we're having in one of our departments," the head of HR informed me as we sat in her office. "It seems that one of our managers has been a bit . . . abrupt with his staff, and even though we moved him to a different position and brought in a new manager, his staff haven't quite . . . moved on." She seemed a bit uncomfortable as she spoke and careful to choose the correct wording.

"Could you give me an example or two?" I asked.

"Well, his new position requires him to go to a monthly meeting hosted by the department he was in charge of, and apparently some of his former staff lock themselves in the bathroom and refuse to come out from well before the meeting and until the meeting is over and he has left the area is one example . . . lots of crying on the day of those meetings . . ."

"Oh, wow," I said. "He sounds like a really scary bully. Why did you place him in a position that still keeps him around?" I asked. "Why didn't you fire him?"

"Well," she answered, "management . . . we ah . . . wanted to promote him."

"What?" I asked, aghast.

She rushed, "Because, after all, he did run a tight ship. We didn't want to lose him . . . and that was the only relevant position."

"Wow," I said. "You guys need a different consultant."

MISUSING MANAGERIAL POWER

Managerial power gets misused in the workplace far more often than we realize.

In a 2007 survey, a quarter of US employees reported having been bullied in the workplace, but the real number was no doubt much higher as many such cases were underreported. Indeed, *Forbes* reported that "a new 2019 Monster.com survey found that nearly 94 percent out of 2,081 employees who participated said they had been bullied in the workplace."[1]

Can you imagine? Grown people made to suffer the kinds of indignities kids do in junior high. Actually, given the statistics, you probably can imagine all too well. It is breathtaking to consider that every day, millions of Americans are shouted at, belittled in front of colleagues, harassed, and picked on.

The reason there are so many such complaints is the old adage: power corrupts. It doesn't matter if you wield it as a shift supervisor or a C-suite executive. Everyone is vulnerable to its impact.

To converse about the potential effects of power requires us to admit we and our values might be fallible in certain situations, so there is huge widespread natural resistance to even discuss the topic. Yet, abusing power is a phenomenon that is so extensive and so damaging to people that it is now (and always should have been) a vital issue that needs to be addressed in all companies—however unpopular it is to do so.

It's important to recognize how power affects people, what gets influenced by power, and what changes with power. It's also important to understand the gradual psychological processes that enable power dynamics to alter people's perceptions, cognitions, and behaviors—and how fast these processes can start their insidious influence on us. And finally, it's crucial to understand what individuals and workplaces can do to counter power's negative effects and whose responsibility it is to put these countermeasures into action.

My personal experience with this scourge peaked in 2015 when I was called in to consult with Israel's chief of police after eight highly publicized and embarrassing instances of abuse of power by its most senior members over the course of a single year. The task was monumental—to help bring about a deep and profound organizational cultural change that would drastically reduce incidents of sexual harassment and other abuses of power throughout all ranks in the 60,000 strong national police force. Reading the latest research on the subject and revisiting some of the older research, I was blown away by the breadth, depth, and severity of the influence that power has on humans.

In a recent study, 45 percent of American workers reported that they had experienced workplace discrimination and/or harassment in the preceding year.[2]

POWER CHANGES ALL PEOPLE
AND FOR THE WORSE

Power does change people. Not could but does change people. The only uncertainty is how soon and to what degree.

Power (not necessarily a lot of power) causes gradual but significant drops in patience, empathy, compassion,[3] noticing the suffering of others,[4] and being willing to accept or even receive feedback.[5] Power also causes increases in excessive self-confidence, sense of immunity from sanctions,[6] and stereotypical thinking.[7] For some, power might even lead to illegal or corrupt actions. But, more commonly, at least in the workplace, power leads to a deterioration in our treatment of others.

Since most of us tend to think of ourselves as good, moral, and honest people, we're likely to believe power could not or has not changed us. But that is precisely what makes power so insidious—it makes us unaware we're doing something wrong.

It is not unusual to twist and distort our perceptions and interpretations of events in order to justify our actions (for example, "Yeah, I yelled a bit loudly, but if that's what it takes to get through to him, it'll help him avoid the same mistake in the future").

We humans are capable of twisting our own interpretation of reality in order to fit our psychological needs so easily that we can justify, ignore, misunderstand, repress, and downright deny our own actions to alarming degrees. These reality-twisting mechanisms, called *psychological defenses*, occur outside our immediate consciousness, allowing us to continue to think of ourselves as good, moral, and honest. They are extremely effective. So much so that despite the damage of power abuse and its extensive prevalence, you will be hard-pressed to find a more unpopular subject.

Most people and companies hate the topic, turn on the denial switch, and refuse to live up to their responsibilities. Senior managers, those with the most power, often view the subject as irrelevant to them or a trifling issue that HR should address. They even find the idea that they themselves might be culprits of bullying and harassment as highly offensive. Ironically, often senior managers react to their indignation at the thought they are bullies by belittling, bullying, and harassing the unfortunate individual who brought up the idea.

The Psychological Processes That Cause Power Abuse

There are a few psychological processes that cause power to have a stunningly wide and negative impact on our capabilities and behaviors.

In the previous chapter, I described the psychological journey of becoming a senior manager and how senior managers develop defense mechanisms that gradually degrade their capacity for empathy, compassion, and noticing the suffering of others. I equated a gradual increase in power to a rising elevator that causes a gradual decline in the clarity with which those with power view others.

However, there is a different psychological process that causes people with power to undergo further changes to their behavior and personality. They gradually lose their willingness to act on feedback, and as time goes on, to even receive feedback. Their self-confidence and hubris increase to levels that are so excessive that they may develop a strong sense of immunity to sanctions. These changes result in a distinct and dangerous decrease in the ability of others to curtail or influence problematic decisions and actions by the people in power. Neither subordinates nor peers can get through at this point because the people in power believe that they just know better.

This is a scary state of affairs that has the potential to endanger the people in power as well as many others. The psychological process causing these changes works like this: Imagine that you are promoted at work, and now you are a team leader in charge of 10 employees.

Immediately, you are the one that determines workloads, schedules, and shifts, and you also have a say regarding promotions, bonuses, and other occasional perks. In other words, all of a sudden, you have power over the 10 employees in your team, and every one of them knows it.

Some will cheer you on because you have a friendly and warm relationship with them and they're happy for you. In all probability, a few will be just a bit nicer and friendlier to you than before. One or two of them might compliment you and congratulate you on your promotion with a dash of extra praise. I'm not talking full-blown sucking up here but, rather, small subtle changes, barely noticeable if at all, by either side.

It might even feel weird at the beginning, and indeed many people freshly promoted have "imposter syndrome"—they still feel, at first, just like a regular employee, the same as they were prior to their sudden promotion to manager. But because it takes longer to change your self-identity than it does to accept a promotion, you initially might feel like an imposter—hence the name.

But gradually you adapt your self-identity and accept that you have been promoted because you are worthy—and, indeed, more worthy than the people you now manage because it was you who was chosen, not them. Your daily interactions with your team members change. Their slightly more positive behavior toward you gradually reinforces your feelings, making your ego believe that you are indeed just a smidgeon more worthy than they are, at least when it comes to your workplace.

At first, the slightly warmer treatment and regard have little effect. But these interactions can happen tens of times a day, hundreds of times a month, so as time goes by, your very slight feelings of superiority will gradually intensify, especially if you keep getting promoted. And the higher up you go, the more power you wield, the more positive regard you will get, and the more smiles you will receive. You will be complimented and even openly admired.

Your self-confidence grows. You no longer feel like an imposter or that you're not worthy to be a manager. Instead, you believe you're really talented, good at your job, smart, and successful.

A gradual perceptual divide starts to form between you and the people below you. You indeed came from their ranks, but you no longer belong or identify with people in those ranks. They don't have all the information that is at your disposal, they don't possess enough pieces of the puzzle to build a correct picture, and they lack the experience you have.

When you were just promoted for the first time, you welcomed feedback, glad to have the opportunity to improve and justify your being selected. But after a while you find yourself partially rejecting some feedback that is given by people who plainly don't know what you know and who can't see what you see. It's different up on the higher rungs of the ladder of success, and people below you can have good intentions, but they don't shoulder the heavy responsibilities you do, and they cannot see the full picture your elevated station provides you. In essence, you come to believe that they perhaps lack the capacity to really provide any useful guidance at all. So gradually, the more your self-confidence grows, your willingness to listen to feedback from the people below you slowly dissipates.

On the other hand, you can't really listen to feedback from your lofty peers because, at this stage, you're competing with them for the ever-diminishing number of higher spots in the company. After all, the pyramid gets narrow at the top. And asking for help and guidance from your superiors might cause them to think that you are unprepared for further promotion or lack self-confidence or that you have reached the top of your capabilities—so you avoid doing that.

This slow and gradual psychological process can strip you of the ability to accept or even listen to feedback. It can cause your self-confidence to tip to excessive levels, rendering you unable to imagine that you might be wrong and making you feel so aloof and superior that you develop a dangerous sense of immunity to sanctions. Your hubris makes you blind to warnings and red flags, just as it causes you to forget that it's just a job and that you're just a person, not necessarily a better or worse human than anybody else, just someone empowered to make workplace decisions.

We have expressions to warn us about becoming too self-important, such as "Don't let success get to your head," because as humans, we have been battling with the negative and dangerous effects of power for many millennia. When Roman emperors and generals returned from successful campaigns and had a parade in their honor, it was customary to have a slave stand behind them on the chariot whispering "*Memento mori*," Latin for "Remember death." In other words, "You're a mortal like everyone else. Don't let success go to your head." Even back then, power, and the hubris that often accompanies it, was considered dangerous to the wielder, but far more dangerous to the people over whom it was held.

Power Corrupts Surprisingly Quickly, Even in Small Doses

The best demonstration of how quickly power can corrupt and cause people to behave in ways that they wouldn't dream of before they were given their power is the Stanford Prison Experiment (SPE). Conducted by psychology professor Richard Zimbardo in 1971, SPE was designed to explore the dynamics between prisoners and their guards.

Volunteers for the experiment were screened to ensure that they were all psychologically stable and healthy. By the flip of a coin, the 24 participants were divided into one group of prisoners and one group of guards. A few university offices were transformed into "cells," guards were provided with appropriate clothing, and prisoners were provided with uncomfortable gowns and wore a chain on one ankle. Prisoners were "arrested" from their homes. Guards had batons and dark glasses—all for the sake of realism and science. Zimbardo himself was the prison superintendent as well as the chief researcher. The experiment was filmed and was well documented. It was later portrayed in the 2015 film *The Stanford Prison Experiment*.

Guards started abusing prisoners within hours. After a day and a half, one prisoner was acting "crazy" and was released from the prison and the experiment. The guards' abuse of the rest of the prisoners grew alarmingly quickly. The prisoners (fellow students) were made to go naked in order to degrade them, were forced to sleep on a cold concrete floor, and were placed in solitary confinement.

All the while, Professor Zimbardo, a psychologist and an expert on the misuse of power, watched while doing nothing to alleviate the suffering of innocents that was being caused by his own decree. On day 6, out of a planned 14-day experiment, a graduate student (whom Zimbardo later married) visited, was horrified, and demanded that Zimbardo end the experiment, which he promptly did.

To my mind, the most telling thing about this highly controversial experiment wasn't the ease and swiftness with which the guards started abusing their fellow students (the inmates) but rather, the ease and rapidity with which the power of being a prison superintendent caused a professor of psychology to totally lose track of his moral compass. Power corrupts quickly and widely, and unfortunately it can hold thrall even over those versed in its insidious ways.

In a recent well-funded experiment, students at a European university were introduced to a game in which the "dictators" could decide how to distribute money following a group task while choosing one out of three options. Two distribution options allocated the money evenly among the team members (with one option allocating a slightly larger sum to the dictators than the other team members). In the third distribution option, the "antisocial" one, the dictators kept most of the money for themselves.

Prior to the experiment, when asked to consider the game theoretically, only 3.3 percent of participants said that they would choose the antisocial distribution if they were chosen to be the dictators. In other words, a vast majority of people recognized the nature of, and shunned, the unfair distribution option in which the leaders abuse their power and keep money that should be distributed to the rest of the team. But all this was in theory.

The experiment itself was conducted a while later with real money, and dictators who chose to abuse power could potentially walk away with $50 to $100—a huge sum for these kinds of experiments. And when it came to the real game played for real money, things transpired differently. Even though when asked theoretically, 97 percent of the subjects had advocated the nonabusive options of distributing the money, over 80 percent of the subjects actually chose the antisocial, power-abusing option at the expense of the rest of their team.

In simple terms, 80 percent of people abused their power to the hilt the minute they got it, acting in the complete opposite way that they themselves had said they would before they were given power. And their subordinates paid the price, as subordinates do in these circumstances, in the form of being treated unfairly and being denied their deserved share of the payout.

Why the Negative Effects of Power Are So Resilient to Change

Power acts swiftly and widely, changing people's perceptions, cognitions, and behaviors and degrading their regard and treatment of others. The degree of these changes varies greatly, but usually the longer people are in power and the more power they have, the larger its negative influence becomes.

For many, the changes will be slow and subtle, but it can gradually transform others into tyrants and bullies. The effects of power are so strong and compelling, they are a damaging part of every work environment and must be addressed.

However, the Catch-22 of power is that those influenced most by it are the only people who can officially decide to address it. And because power changes perceptions and cognitions, those in power seldom realize that their treatment and regard of others has degraded. They don't realize that they are causing people unnecessary emotional pain, and they usually aren't open to or willing to hear feedback. As far as they are concerned, there's no problem, and nothing in this regard needs to change. Power's Catch-22 is a significant part of the reason so many people suffer from work-related harassment and bullying together with the anxiety, stress, and unhappiness that invariably accompany the recipients of such treatment.

The good news is that the negative effects of power in the workplace can be tackled and minimized if the people in charge realize that it's prudent to do so. However, they must possess the right values, leadership skills, and plenty of grit to galvanize the others with power in their organization to follow suit (the Israeli chief of police back in 2015 happily had all three in abundance).

HOW TO MINIMIZE THE EFFECTS OF POWER IN THE WORKPLACE

In order to minimize the negative effects of power in organizations, it is necessary to implement an anti-power plan and make it a permanent part of the corporate culture. It can't just be an HR initiative. It must originate from and have the full support of top management.

True prevention requires a clear plan that includes all levels of the organization. I recommend following these principles.

Make People Aware and Educate

Because the subject of managerial power is so unpopular, many managers lack a good understanding of the dangers of power, the way it influences and changes us, how it degrades our regard of others, and why it makes us impervious to feedback. So, the first thing that's important to do is introduce the subject and educate managers about the nature of the beast, so to speak.

A word of warning: when educating coworkers about an unpopular subject, make sure to keep it interesting by using movies in which the gradual negative effects of power can be witnessed (for instance, *The Stanford Prison Experiment* or *J. Edgar*) or by presenting interesting research. Steer well away from using current political figures as examples because, if you point to those examples, things can get ugly quickly and the entire point will be lost.

Keep the Discussion Ongoing

In the 1960s, people went to the beach and applied "suntan lotion" in order to get a better tan. After we realized that using suntan lotion is akin to holding a sign that says, "Melanomas R Us" (melanomas are life-threatening skin cancers), we not only stopped using suntan lotion but we also started using strong anti-UV light creams to protect our skin whenever we were spending lengthy periods outdoors. The sun's UV rays are dangerous, constant, and everywhere. If you're outside, you can't really escape them. You can only be aware of their danger and do certain things to protect yourself from their dangerous effects, even though you don't directly feel or perceive any negative immediate effects.

The sun's UV light effects are akin to the negative effects of power. These negative effects are constant and everywhere—you can't escape them once you are in a position of power. But once you are aware of their dangers, there are certain things that you can do to protect yourself. Just as you should apply protection against UV light every time you need to be out in the sun, protecting yourself and your organization from the dangers of power is an ongoing affair that must be discussed, again and again, even though many will find the topic unpopular or even offensive.

Many people can't imagine that they'll ever abuse their power ("Why do you think I'll turn into a bully? I won't!"). The sad reality is, power can make people do things they never would have done before. Constant reminders and training are essential for everyone.

Discuss the Dangers of Hubris

When people use the expression "Don't let success go to your head," they mean it as a warning—it's similar to "*Memento mori*" and "Beware the sin of hubris" in meaning. People who let success go to their head become complacent, overconfident, and proud. They stop listening to others and view others as lesser people than themselves—which is never smart. In the reality show *Survivor*, whenever you hear contestants bragging about how well they are doing and in what a great strategic position they're in, that's usually indicative of a huge blind spot, and they find themselves voted out, with an unused immunity token or two still in their pocket.

We can also be subject to blind spots in the workplace. For example, people can suddenly find themselves surpassed on the organization chart by someone who once was their subordinate (General George Patton being overtaken by General Omar Bradley comes to mind). But more often, the price managers pay for their power-based hubris is that they lose the goodwill of those below them, as well as their input, ideas, and willingness to put in effort. They also lose touch with many things that are beneath their lofty notice, rendering them ineffective as managers, unaware and unable to react to developments that have important bearings on their own success as well as the company's.

Adopt Habits to Keep Yourself Well Grounded

In order to remain well grounded, remind yourself and the managers below you that true self-confidence runs quiet (when you really know your worth, there's no need to constantly solicit praise from others). True leadership does not require the use of force or intimidation, and seniority doesn't make you a better human being.

I strongly recommend adopting a habit or two to further rein-force the grounding effect—little things that will nonetheless make a difference. For example, eat lunch with your subordinates once every few days, chat with them, and make it a point to know some-thing about their personal lives. Make coffee every now or then for the people who regularly make you coffee. Every so often let some-one on your team park in your good parking space and you park in theirs. Remain humble when successful by praising subordinates who contributed, not yourself. When failing, learn a lesson yourself, and tell others about what you learned before making others learn from their mistakes.

Always Keep a "No-Person" (the Opposite of a "Yes-Man" or "Yes-Person") Close

People in power can gradually lose patience with subordinates who tend to disagree with them, and over time, they can find themselves surrounded by people who always agree with whatever they say or do—the proverbial yes-person.

To counteract that tendency, everyone in power needs to keep around someone who is the opposite of a yes-person, someone who speaks truth to power, someone who will argue with them and point out unworthy behaviors—in other words, a no-person. The no-person's job is to counter the negative effects of power by pointing out instances in which their boss acted with arrogance, didn't listen enough, bullied subordinates (used their power to coerce or intimi-date someone weaker), and exhibited other negative manifestations of the effects of power. The better the no-person is at their job, the less they will be needed in that role because the negative effects of power are much easier to acknowledge and control when they are still weak.

Start at the Top, and Lead from the Front

Limiting the negative effects of power is of course a top-down affair. Senior managers need to put the subject on the table and keep it there. They should make it a point to treat everyone with respect and model the behaviors they expect from others by using their managerial power in decision-making, not when interacting with people (don't worry, no one will forget who's in charge).

When modeling, follow the *rule of dilution*, which is that 75 percent of what you model will be mirrored downward to the next line of managers, and 75 percent of what they model will be mirrored to the people under them. So, be strict with yourself.

Curbing the negative effects of managerial power is a task that requires more leadership than management. Managers get things done. They conduct behavior and output. Leaders conduct emotions. They make people feel safe, worthy, and respected. And by so doing, they positively motivate people, which helps to grow the organization's bottom line.

Leaders who generate anxiety and fear of speaking up, who stifle ideas, and cause their subordinates to feel worthless and unworthy are leaders who are failing at their job. They aren't utilizing all available resources to make their company successful because they are tapping into only a fraction of the available human energy and brainpower at their disposal. It's just as mistaken (or stupid) as baking a cake using only some of the ingredients in the recipe, even though you actually have all them right there. If all the (people) resources are needed, if all are willing to contribute, and if all are at your disposal, then please use them all fully.

Ultimately, leaders who have let power go to their heads are placing their company in danger. Cutting themselves off from important information and recommendations that their subordinates have learned to keep to themselves could set themselves and their company up for blind spots that otherwise could have been anticipated.

Build Leadership Around Values, Modesty, and Caring

Some leaders are great orators, some have a magnetic physical presence and a born air of superiority, some have the kind of charisma that can inspire or instill a spark of fear in the eyes of the people they lead. Those are attributes some people are lucky enough to be born with.

While most of us are not so lucky, I contend that many people can become true leaders by acquiring, refining, and adopting leadership attributes and skills over time. Adopting values of modesty and equality and wielding weapons of fairness, kindness, and caring toward the people who work for you will turn you into a leader in their eyes, and eventually in your own.

When people are feeling secure, wanted, and appreciated, I believe they give their best, so leaders should strive to make people feel secure, wanted, and appreciated in advance, in order that they have the best chances of success from the beginning. I believe kindness and caring breed happiness and a sense of belonging and that the more people feel that way, the less they will be willing to live without it (even for more pay or a chance of promotion).

People in a position of power that follow these guidelines will eventually see a spark in the eyes of the people around them. It won't be a spark of fear, but rather a spark of inspiration. And everyone around them, as well as themselves, will have a happier and more successful life for it.

Don't Add Unnecessary and Unethical "Sticks" to Your Managerial Toolbox

Managers have many tools at their disposal in corporate America when it comes to encouraging their team to perform well.

They obviously have the full array of "carrots" at their disposal. When employees do well, managers can afford those subordinates extra smiles of warmth and positive regard. They can congratulate them, praise them in front of the team, write them a letter of excellence, and recommend they get a bonus, promotion, or higher wages. They can leave a little chocolate on their subordinates' desks with a note of appreciation or send the chocolates home, so the employees' family can be proud as well.

They also have the full array of "sticks" at their disposal, which they can use when subordinates provide a lackluster effort. They can frown at them, act disappointed, meet with them and chastise them for lack of effort, they can write a negative review, delay promotion or pay raise, give an official reprimand, or even recommend the subordinate be dismissed.

All in all, managers have quite a few managerial tools at their disposal in the realms of carrots and sticks. So, it's both strange and upsetting to me that so many managers take it upon themselves to add other types of sticks that are not only uncalled for but also entail emotionally damaging actions that are antithetical to effective management.

For example, belittling employees in the presence of their peers or harassing, bullying, and even ignoring them is not only detrimental to their future performance but it is also totally unethical. A manager has no right to act that way toward an adult employee, or toward any human being for that matter.

Just as managers cannot attack employees physically, they should not be allowed to attack employees emotionally. In many cases, the pain of an emotional attack lasts longer and causes more damage than a physical attack—so, in that sense, it's actually worse than a physical attack.

It's unheard of for managers to enhance their "carrot toolbox" by unethical means, for instance, by offering out-of-pocket personal bribes to employees who perform well. So, why are managers allowed to bolster their "sticks toolbox" with emotionally damaging and unethical behaviors and actions? While such behaviors and actions are formally not allowed throughout much of corporate America, the fact of the matter is that they are often displayed by senior managers.

There is an elephant in the rooms
of corporate America: power abuse.

Emotional abuse is allowed, in fact, for many reasons. First, physical scars are always easier to see than emotional ones. To a large degree, physical abuse is regarded as crossing a line (it's actually illegal) while emotional abuse is not regarded in the same way. In other words, physical abuse is no longer the norm, but emotional abuse still is.

But the main fault for so many of us being unhappy at work and victimized by emotional abuse is our own. We are the ones who tolerate it and remain silent. Many of us have grown so used to the stench of various levels of emotional abuse at work that we just don't let it register strongly enough when we encounter it.

We chalk it up to our boss having a bad day, we even kind of expect it, or we consider ourselves lucky when our boss turns out to be friendly and nice. When things do register, our fear of being labeled a "troublemaker" or even being fired often serves to silence us externally, while internally, our inaction often causes us to pay a price in various forms of lowered psychological well-being. We hate it, but wielding little power ourselves, what can we as individuals do?

DON'T BE DISHEARTENED

This has been a tough chapter to write, and I'm sure a tough chapter to read. The abuse of power and the pain it inflicts on others in the workplace is a sobering reminder of how far we still have to go to create work environments where everyone feels safe and inspired to do their best.

I believe there are signs that things are getting better.

The effects of Covid-19 on labor shortages have been painfully felt by many countries. But to some degree, supply chain issues caused by shortages of drivers, warehouse personnel, and other key positions have, in fact, brought us even closer to our global goals of social justice for employment underdogs.

Many of these labor shortages can, in fact, be easily filled by all the out-of-work immigrants, ex-felons, and people with disabilities—employment underdogs whom we, as a society, constantly overlook. If we learned anything during the pandemic, it's that we need everyone. This is exactly the time we can start winning—the time for underdogs to enter the mainstream.

Please don't get disheartened by the dismal state of affairs in our places of work. I started this book by claiming that most people don't realize how close we are to social justice. We're truly getting there.

Part III proves that claim by describing what corporate America's responsibilities are in regard to social justice and then what each of us can and should do to help corporate America lead the transformation of our workplaces into warm, caring, diverse, and fully inclusive environments that are worthy of our best efforts and motivations. For these goals to be met and meaningful change to transpire, you will be called on to risk nothing more than a few seconds a day of your time. Used wisely and widely, those few seconds will suffice to create the changes that will make each and every one of us a happier person.

All you need to do to contribute to this change, this underdog revolution, is provide a little nudge to corporate America.

PART III

GETTING FROM
HERE TO THERE

9

Reserved Employment for the Opportunity-Deprived

If just 1 percent more of people with disabilities joined the US labor force, the US GDP could get a boost of up to $25 billion.[1]

The two challenges of getting everyone into the workforce are (1) bias-based workplace discrimination and (2) job availability.

BIAS

There used to be a time (basically until World War II) that working was considered an endeavor mainly suited for males, especially at jobs that needed brains and skill. As recently as 1970, only 1 percent of dentists, 8 percent of physicians, and 5 percent of lawyers in the US were women.

Fifty years ago, the de facto misogynist culture of the day viewed women as less suited or less able than men physically, cognitively, and emotionally in many occupations and sports. Sadly, many women of great talent bought into that male-serving ethos and never tried to utilize their talents or develop careers.

But, oh, how far have we come! Fifty years later, anyone stating publicly that women are less able than men in any regard does so at their own peril and is guaranteed a well-deserved large and vocal public backlash.

An optimist might discern a trend. It seems that we humans are slowly outgrowing our baffling, biased tendency to disregard various groups of people just because of their gender, ethnicity, color, or other biased-based categories. Perhaps the folly and bigotry of the past is behind us and at long last all people can be viewed as potential resources to companies and organizations—thus, giving everyone a fair chance to join the workforce and become a contributing member of society.

Well, the good news is that when zooming out to larger trends, over the past 50 years or so, we have definitely witnessed positive global change regarding equality and inclusion. However, when zooming in to magnify current workplace practices and realities, it's clear we still have many biases we need to get rid of.

Workplace Discrimination in the United States

The findings of a meta-analysis of work discrimination studies in the United States over the past 25 years are sadly disappointing. With the rise in popularity of DE&I, with a growing social movement that is helped by the internet and social media, with so many people voicing outrage over social injustices—with all these changes and forces aligned, how much better do you think things are?[2] Can you guess the degree of positive change in racial hiring discrimination between 1989 and 2017 that the study found?

None. Zero.

Workplace Discrimination in Europe

In a late 2020 report, the Organization for Economic Co-operation and Development (OECD), which consists of 38 countries, stated that one of its key challenges was to ensure "that OECD countries are equipped to make the most of diversity by fully utilizing all talent among diverse populations and promoting inclusive labor markets." The report considered five key groups that are still "widely considered disadvantaged in the labor market and society at large and who often face discrimination based on their group membership: immigrants, their descendants and ethnic minorities; LGBTQ people; older people; people with disabilities; and women."[3]

It seems that the positive trend I mentioned earlier constitutes primarily just talk. Little actual progress has been made. In the United States, Europe, and in most of the rest of the world, various large populations still endure workplace discrimination, exclusion, and inequity, while suffering the ensuing emotional scars that continued prejudice creates.

> Ending bias and discrimination against someone doesn't erase old scars. It just stops creating new ones.

Again and again, I find that governments, societies, and individuals focus (correctly) on trying to end discrimination because they believe (incorrectly) that once discrimination ends, all will be well.

As I have shown in previous chapters, long-term discrimination can create trauma and various psychological scars that don't magically disappear once their cause is removed. These scars can cause people to lose confidence, to believe that they indeed lack ability, to become anxious, and to underestimate themselves. These psychological wounds can run deep, and they require time, human warmth, and caring to eventually mend.

However, the modern workplace's cold corporate culture is far from patient, and it doesn't allow time or provide human warmth and caring for anybody. Apparently, there's "no crying in baseball,"[4] and there's no crying in corporate America either. So, even if all global discrimination were to end today, many employment underdogs would still struggle to find sustainable work.

THE WRONG EMPLOYMENT OPPORTUNITIES AREN'T OPPORTUNITIES AT ALL

Many entry-level jobs in today's cold corporate culture are immediately demanding, very stressful, and often deprived of human caring and warmth. So, offering such jobs to people whose scars are in need of human warmth in order to heal is just setting them up for failure. And every additional failure extracts a price in the form of lowered self-esteem and self-efficacy, making the next attempt just a bit more difficult.

Some people who have suffered long-term discrimination can't fit into just any job. They need a job that takes their emotional and physical needs into consideration. Sometimes they just need a workplace that can provide warmth, caring, and a bit more patience than usual. As a result, some employment underdogs have fewer employment options at which they can actually succeed than most people. So, even if discrimination and bigotry were magically eradicated forever, there would still be a large group of employment underdogs who wouldn't be able to actually find a job that is accommodating and appropriate to their scarred capabilities and psyche.

JOB AVAILABILITY

There's a suitable job for every unemployed person out there, but it's not always available.

The key word here is "available" because in today's huge global market, a job can be found for any set of scarred capabilities and for practically any kind of disability. The problem is that when unemployed underdogs with limited options look for a job in which they can succeed (regular productivity for regular pay), it is often already staffed by people who have unlimited options.

For example, people with significant hearing disabilities are often chronically unemployed. However, there are many things people with hearing disabilities can do, such as joining a team that provides chat services—which is often an entry-level job and a good place for some people with hearing disabilities to start their employment journey. Plus, many companies provide chat services so there are quite a few chat jobs out there.

The problem is very few companies realize that their chat teams provide them with an opportunity to diversify their workforces by hiring a few people with hearing disabilities. Of the many companies with chat teams that I've met with over the years, only one made a point of hiring people with hearing disabilities. The rest hire people who have many more employment options than people with severe hearing disabilities.

Another example is a call center. Call centers have some jobs that are stressful, emotionally demanding, and entail a lot of persuasion (which people with lowered self-confidence find hard), like sales or rejecting insurance claims. But there are many call-center jobs that are much less stressful and don't entail persuasion at all—jobs that actually require patience and a willingness to help, like assisting people who are less proficient with the internet and online services. Again, very few companies save some of their less emotionally demanding jobs for the unemployed underdogs who need such work in order to jumpstart their employment careers.

REOD: A Simple Concept That Can Change the World

Have you ever questioned the need for reserved parking for people with disabilities? I assume not. Because at this point in history, it makes perfect sense (albeit, it wasn't entirely obvious when it was first instituted). In fact, the concept of reserved parking for people with disabilities is nowadays accepted worldwide.

It's true that the rest of us would also like to park close to the entrance of wherever we're going—but we can in fact park farther away and walk. So, we save some of the close parking spaces for those of us who don't have the option to park farther away because if we didn't, they would forever be stuck in their homes. It's a simple concept really that makes immediate sense to most of us.

In fact, we often get upset when we see someone who's obviously able-bodied parking in a reserved parking spot, and many countries have "shaming websites" where pictures of offenders and their license plates are posted and thoroughly trashed by talkbacks. So, globally, societies reserve specific parking spots for people who have mobility issues so that they can access the same places everyone else can because if they can't park close to their destination, they are imprisoned in their homes, and that just isn't fair.

The concept of Reserved Employment for the Opportunity Deprived (REOD) is very similar to the concept of reserved parking, with just three small changes: exchange parking spots with jobs, mobility issues with opportunity-deprived people, and places with the workforce. This is what you get: we, as a society, reserve specific jobs for opportunity-deprived people so that they can access the workforce like everybody else. Otherwise, they are imprisoned in their homes, and that just isn't fair. If it's globally accepted and embraced when it comes to parking, should it not be globally accepted and embraced when it comes to employment?

Imagine

Imagine that the whole world decides that employment is as important as parking and we embrace the concept of REOD with the same fervor we apply to reserved parking. Noncompliant employers would be called out on social media. Family members of employment underdogs would write and complain to their own employer's HR that there is a job ideal for their unemployed family member and should be reserved for them or for people with similar needs.

The financial effects of the global unemployed workforce changing status from zero productivity to regular productivity would be dramatic, to say the least, and it would have a huge positive impact on us all. If employing just 1 percent of the unemployed people with disabilities in the United States is worth $25 billion to the economy, then getting all the unemployed people with disabilities in the United States to join the labor force would be a massive boon to the economic good fortunes of all of us.

Moreover, the Covid-19 pandemic demonstrated that people's productivity does not go down when working from home, so there are even more opportunities to hire and reserve jobs for unemployed underdogs who need to stay at home because of a disability or because they have to care for family members.

Imagine. It's just a small social norm away.

BEYOND IMAGINING: REAL COMPANIES THAT EMBRACE THE CONCEPT OF REOD

There are companies that actually believe that their values should influence their business practices, and these companies walk their diversity talk with integrity. They are truly deserving of a much bigger spotlight than I can provide.

Walgreens Boots Alliance (WBA)

The Walgreens Boots Alliance has made inclusion a core company value. It makes a point to hire people with various kinds of disabilities, pay them regular wages, and assist them in reaching regular productivity. It has even taken the applaudable step of including DE&I as a bonus criterion for managers!

Lemon Tree Hotels (LTH)

Lemon Tree Hotels is perhaps the best example of a large, global, free-market company (over 5,000 employees) that epitomizes everything I have been advocating in this book. It has taken the concept of reserve employment to new levels entirely. And its values of equality, diversity, and assuming the responsibility of the strong to safeguard the weak—all of these values dictate its business decisions and actions.

Not surprisingly, Lemon Tree's business outcomes have soared in concert with these policies. It's the truest and most shinning beacon of what humanity and the modern workplace should aspire to. But despite Lemon Tree's noble approach to embracing employment underdogs, most people are unaware of the company. Lemon Tree acts with true humility, and (unlike so many other companies) the company prefers DE&I walk over DE&I talk.

Lemon Tree was founded by Patu Keswani in 2004. Patu was educated as an electrical engineer with postgraduate training in business management. He acquired his knowledge of the hotel business working for the TATA Group as senior vice president and as chief operating officer of the Taj Group of Hotels.

I had the pleasure of interviewing Patu and Aradhana Lal (Lemon Tree Hotels' vice president of brand, communications, and sustainability initiatives). First off, I asked Patu to tell me his origin story regarding inclusion. I'm always interested in people's motivations and the sparks that ignite them, and I was wondering what motivated an electrical engineer to start what has become (to my knowledge) the most inclusive large free-market business on the planet. This is how things transpired.

Seeing Value in the Hearing Impaired

A few years after its founding, Lemon Tree Hotels secured a large investment aimed at accelerating its growth. With the need to bring on many new employees, Patu requested his HR manager to find and hire two hearing-impaired employees, and then he promptly forgot about it.

Patu was reminded of it two years later when a woman of little means, obviously dressed in her best clothes and carrying a bouquet of flowers, asked for a short meeting with him. She had come to thank him for saving her son's life and to invite him to her son's wedding as she was the mother of one of the two people with hearing loss Patu had asked HR to hire.

She explained that without a job, her son could never marry because he was not financially viable. But after two years of work, her son had not only gained steady employment, he had also gained confidence and had ended the social isolation chronic unemployment often brings. He was now ready to marry and start his own family.

Patu's willingness to hire two hearing-impaired people had far greater implications for the two employees than just getting a job. In effect, he opened a door that enabled them to enjoy normal lives.

Realizing the dramatic effect that an entry-level job could have on those who are opportunity deprived, Patu immediately asked HR to grow the number of hearing-impaired employees to 100.

As more hearing-impaired people began working at Lemon Tree, the company quickly discovered that hearing-impaired room attendants were about 15 percent more efficient and productive than their able-bodied counterparts. They were less distracted, on the one hand (having no auditory "chatting" distractions), and, on the other hand, they were more engaged and motivated to make the best of the opportunity they were awarded. Their disability, coupled with the right job, actually gave them an "extra ability" in performing those jobs versus able-bodied people. That got Patu thinking.

Hiring People with Down Syndrome

Dining steward jobs entail two different components: (1) a low-skill repetitive component (which most stewards hate and find boring) that involves making up the tables and the buffet presentations, which demands precision, and (2) more difficult components, such as explaining the menu, taking orders, and up-selling by offering guests additional drinks and dishes (which most stewards like to do).

Patu decided to divide the job of restaurant steward into two parts. To perform the repetitive and precision-demanding job, he decided to hire people with Down syndrome, while able-bodied employees would perform the other parts of the job. In essence, he created a situation in which each of his relevant employee groups enjoyed their work much more than previously. The new employees with Down syndrome were thrilled to be employed (and paid) just like able-bodied people. And the other stewards were rid of the component of their job that they most disliked, so they could focus on the two parts they did enjoy.

At the time I wrote this book, Opportunity Deprived Indians (ODIs) composed 20 percent of Lemon Tree Hotels' employees. Thousands of others worked in the company for a few years, and then moved on.

Lemon Tree's work with ODIs has grown to include many other opportunity-deprived groups. For instance, they built a two-year training program for 16-year-old orphans, which enables the orphans to easily find jobs when they reach the age of 18 when they have to leave the orphanage to fend for themselves. (Without such training, many orphans when reaching 18 find themselves on the streets as beggars or prostitutes.)

Lemon Tree also partnered with the government to accrue most of the orphans' wages until they are released at the age of 18, so that graduates of the program receive a lump sum of money with which to start their independent lives.

Lately, Lemon Tree has begun to hire acid victims (people who were attacked with acid with the intention to kill, disfigure, maim, or torture—mainly, but not only, women), a step many other managers from the hospitality industry would balk at due to the prominent disfiguring such attacks often cause. However, Patu and LTH figured that precisely because so many employers balked at hiring disfigured employees, especially in the hospitality industry, that acid survivors deserved to be awarded with at least one workplace safe haven.

A disfigured person on the inside is a person like anybody else, so imagine how it feels to be constantly looked at with disgust and revulsion, day after day. How insurmountably difficult it would be to keep one's self-worth and self-confidence in these circumstances and what a godsend and life changer LTH are to these people.

The Positive Effects of the ODI Hiring Policy on LTH's Bottom Line

Even though at the onset, some of the hotels' regular employees didn't connect fully to Patu's initiative, the positive effects of hiring employment underdogs quickly took root. When 20 percent of employees are employee underdogs, the other 80 percent of employees get to interact with them every day. So very quickly, what started out as Patu's initiative, touched everyone, moved everyone, and became everyone's project.

Managers were taught an additional language—Indian sign language. Able-bodied stewards learned to work alongside their counterpart stewards with Down syndrome and to interact with them properly. Seeing people with prominent disabilities became commonplace, enabling the able-bodied to look beyond the disabilities and to discover the people and personalities that live within.

Employees developed a strong sense of purpose, their engagement soared, and employee attrition rates were halved. As Aradhana explained: "When you're inclusive, the sense of fulfillment is in a new order."

To this day, Lemon Tree Hotels' employees are filled with a sense of purpose and pride, which is mirrored in the various slogans their wonderful and unique culture has generated: "We feel pride when they no longer hide," or "When life takes its toll, we try to make them whole."

LTH's Core Values

I've lamented previously about the lack of regard corporations have for their own, publicly stated, values. As we've seen, most companies' values mainly serve the stockholders. They aren't known by the rank and file; they are not believed by other employees; and management doesn't invest any more personal effort in the company's corporate social responsibilities than writing the occasional check. It's interesting to see how a company like Lemon Tree Hotels, in comparison, defines and acts upon their values.

These are Lemon Tree Hotels' values as they appear on their website:

> **Health and Safety.** We will always focus on ensuring the health, safety, security, and well-being of all our stakeholders, including the communities within which we operate our business:
>
> - *Teamwork:* We recognize that superlative performance is always the result of teamwork.
>
> - *Ownership:* We always take responsibility for our actions.
>
> - *Respect and empathy:* We always exhibit respect and concern for colleagues, guests, and partners.
>
> - *Integrity:* We always maintain the highest standards of fairness and transparency in all our dealings.
>
> - *Spirited fun:* We create an exciting and spirited work environment encouraging our colleagues to think freely.
>
> - *Excellence:* We always drive excellence in what we do.[5]

Aligning Actions with Values

Many corporations write checks to various foundations as a major part of their corporate social responsibility (CSR) endeavors, and so does LTH. However, LTH doesn't limit its CSR efforts to "superficial giving." The following are examples of LTH's "profound giving" practices, their above-and-beyond efforts that are not commonplace at all, efforts that reflect their full commitment to their values.

ODIs

By hiring the community's most chronically unemployed underdogs, LTH contributes much to the well-being of their communities. In order to fully integrate its hundreds of ODI employees, LTH makes sure that other employees take an active role in helping ODI employees succeed every day. Thus, in a very real way, each and every one of LTH's employees expresses this core value and contributes to their community's well-being. The success of this program also necessitates and fosters teamwork, ownership, and respect and empathy for others.

Tribal Art

Lemon Tree Hotels is the largest buyer, nationally, of tribal art from the region of Bastar, Madhya Pradesh. The purchases help to support poor tribal artisans in that region and allow LTH to showcase their art extensively across its hotels, thus serving the values of respect and empathy, along with community well-being.

Employee Well-Being

I'm not sure many corporations have a core value that speaks of "spirited fun." I found a lovely example of this value when I heard about their "pooch policy." Each and every hotel adopts a stray dog (or two) and not only feeds them, loves them, and takes care of them but also assigns them various jobs—business card and all.

Bobby (from Lemon Tree Goa), for instance, is in charge of "Horizontal meditation and stillness," while Lemos's business card reads: "Deputy Assistant Associate to the Assistant Deputy Manager reporting to the Executive Assistant to the Chairman." His job is to make management lean. So, it's no surprise that they talk about their employee engagement as "being on a different level."

The Workplace We Deserve

Lemon Tree Hotels practically embodies all the components I've discussed that compose the inclusive safe place our current workplaces need to become:

- Corporate values that cater to the community and employees' well-being

- A safe place of empathy, warmth, and real caring for those less fortunate, creating a workforce that truly mirrors the community's actual diversity

- Transparency regarding sustainability practices and outcomes, including carbon footprints, inclusion, and CSR

Lemon Tree is exceptional—a hospitality business that proudly enables people with emotional and physical scars, or obvious cognitive disabilities, to work and engage with customers in an industry that typically strives for beauty and is intolerant of imperfection.

Shareholders' Delight

Lemon Tree Hotels has won numerous awards and citations, generating much honor and bragging rights for its shareholders. Financially, its social endeavors have had a huge positive effect on the company's bottom line, propelling Lemon Tree Hotels to become the third-largest hotel chain in India in just a few years.

There are many famous jewels that have originated in India: The Koh-i-Noor diamond and the Hope diamond, to name two that are especially well known. I would argue that Lemon Tree Hotels surpasses them all. It is a shining global DE&I beacon of excellence.

CAN REOD CHANGE COME FROM THE TOP OR THROUGH GOVERNMENTAL DECREE?

The likelihood of a future US president signing legislation that required businesses to reserve a certain number of jobs for employment underdogs is unlikely, to say the least. First, the legislation would have to secure majority support from both the Senate and the House of Representatives (good luck with that). Every politician who thought of supporting such a bill would come under intense pressure from corporate America to change their minds.

And lastly, everyone who voted yay would face a huge public outcry and backlash by those who feared the federal government was encroaching on their basic rights regarding freedom and the pursuit of happiness. To successfully take on such a challenge, a future president would need to be endowed with levels of leadership, intelligence, statesmanship, and charisma that have yet to be encountered outside the realm of fantasy.

But the sad reality is that even if such a leader were found, and even if all the above transpired, it would have very little positive impact on underdog employment. You see, reserving jobs for people with lesser opportunities by governmental decree has been done before, more than once, and it doesn't really work.

WHY RESERVED EMPLOYMENT LAWS ARE INEFFECTIVE

I haven't come across reserved employment laws for all opportunity-deprived populations, but quite a few countries have reserved employment laws regarding people with disabilities.

Germany
In Germany, all public or private employers with over 20 employees must reserve 5 percent of their positions for employees who have

a severe disability. The degree of impairment is determined by a list of guidelines, impairments, and diseases. It's a play-or-pay law, with employer fines ranging from 120 to 320 euros per position.

In 2019, there were 171,599 companies in Germany with over 20 employees. Most of them (104,492 businesses) didn't hire enough people with disabilities and preferred to pay the equalization levy.[6]

France

In France, all public or private employers with over 20 employees must reserve 6 percent of their positions for employees with disabilities. As in Germany, noncomplying employers need to pay a fine. The levy equates to 400 times the hourly minimum wage per "missing" disabled employee for organizations with 20 to 199 employees, 500 times the hourly minimum wage for organizations with 501 to 749 employees, and 600 times for organizations with more than 750 employees.

In 2012, only 27 percent of all relevant businesses met the quota fully by directly employing disabled workers.[7] Furthermore, a study from 2016 found that not only did France's Disabled Workers Act fail to improve the employment of people with disabilities, it actually did the opposite: "Our findings highlight *a negative impact* of the Disabled Workers Act on the employment of people with disabilities."[8]

Austria

The quota law requires employers with more than 24 employees to employ 1 registered disabled person (50 percent degree of disability) per 25 employees. In order to count toward the quota, a person must be certified by a medical doctor as having only 50 percent of the work capabilities of a nondisabled person. Companies that fail to meet the quota are liable to pay a compulsory "equalization levy" of at least 238 euros per month.[9]

Other Countries

In Spain, companies with 50 or more employees must reserve at least 2 percent of jobs for workers with disabilities (with an equal to or higher than 33 percent degree of disability). In Italy, the quota is 2 percent, in India 3 percent, in China 1.5 percent, and in Japan, it's 1.8 percent, with a monthly penalty for breach of 50,000 yen.

What all these examples boil down to is that the top-down approach to reserved employment doesn't work. Most organizations prefer to take the hit, pay the fines, and happily continue their exclusion of various employment underdog populations.

We could wait for governments to get it right. France recently (2019) revamped their disability employment laws, so perhaps it (or a different country) will eventually hit on the right formula of quota percentages, fines, disability definitions, and other variables. However, as we wait, the unemployment of disadvantaged people continues to make our weakest weaker, perpetuating our cruel disregard for their plight and abandoning many to miserable battles with health issues, poverty, and social isolation.

Or we could decide not to wait for governments to get it right but rather adopt the bottom-up approach. While it may seem unbelievable to you that we, as individuals, are capable of creating national or international social change, I maintain otherwise.

In the next chapter, I'll introduce you to a few dramatic examples of national social change that started with just a handful of motivated individuals. We, as individuals, are far from powerless, as history shows. We just need to be reminded of this fact every now and again in order for us to act.

The fight for social justice in the workplace starts at the bottom, with individuals and families embracing their power to achieve change and social justice.

10

Change Fueled by Love: The Untapped Power of Family and Friends

We look forward to the time when the
Power of Love will replace the Love of Power.
—William Gladstone,
Prime Minister of the United Kingdom for
12 years, off and on, from 1868 through 1894

I hope you're convinced that social justice in the workplace must start with full inclusion and that it is the responsibility of large corporations to make full inclusion happen on their own—not in response to government edicts.

As discussed in previous chapters, full inclusion is a win for everybody. It improves corporate performance, it helps employment underdogs become economically self-sufficient, it helps mitigate social injustices, and it makes us all happier and healthier individuals.

The data I've provided and the experiences of most people clearly demonstrate that many (if not most) workplaces neglect employees' basic emotional needs of human warmth and caring, thus creating an emotional barrier that makes the modern workplace inaccessible to many. Those who can tolerate working in uncaring emotional environments are often forced to endure abuse, bullying, and a rampant disregard for their need to achieve work-life balance. These cause many, perhaps even most, people currently employed to suffer from various levels of work-related stress, anxiety, and depression.

For all this to change, there are two things we need to discuss. First, we need to understand exactly what we're asking corporations and employers to change and what we want them to actually do. Second, we need to see what each of us can contribute to motivate corporate America (and the rest of the world) to actually embrace the movement and implement these changes.

GETTING FROM HERE TO THERE

Businesses are usually good at setting targets, subtargets, substeps to achieve those targets, establishing work plans, monitoring progress, and rewarding achievements. So, in regard to inclusion, what should large corporations' targets and action items actually be? Because without a clear path of stepping stones to success, without a to-do list leading to the necessary changes, without clear goals for managers to manage, even employers that are truly motivated to better the emotional treatment of their employees will falter.

To answer these questions, I've defined three targets that workplaces can adopt to firmly place themselves on the path to becoming fully inclusive and accessible to all. Success in all three is necessary to transform any workplace to one of caring, integrity, inclusion, and inevitably, better financial results.

First, establish transparency regarding DE&I, which will create motivation for companies to constantly improve their inclusion practices rather than focus on rhetoric. Once companies' actual inclusion practices are laid bare for public consumption, I believe many consumers will reward or penalize them by increasing or withholding their purchases.

Second, adopt the concept of Reserved Employment for the Opportunity Deprived (REOD), which will enable companies to more easily find good employment fits for various employment underdogs in their communities.

Third, transform corporate America's cold and detached culture into a *corporate culture of caring* (CCC), which requires accomplishing two subtargets to achieve:

> *Labeling emotionally hazardous jobs:* If a specific job is emotionally hazardous because of a harassing and domineering manager, lousy work-life balance, or a cold, detached, and uncaring corporate culture, companies can decide to (embarrassingly) apply the label, or they can work with the manager and transform the culture so that the label won't be needed.

> *Adopting top-down accountability:* Make all managerial bonuses contingent on employee well-being and DE&I outcomes, a step that should instill all ranks of an organization with enough motivation to actually bring about change.

Let's examine these targets in a little more detail.

#DIVERSITYLABELS:
TRANSPARENCY REGARDING DE&I

It was just over 30 years ago, in 1990, that the U.S. Department of Agriculture mandated by law that all food companies include a detailed, standardized list of ingredients and a nutrition "facts panel" on their products. The law imposed a cost on companies by demanding that all food companies, large and small, rich or poor, reliably list the ingredients of each of their products on their packaging labels.

Despite the cost for food companies, the law makes great sense, and it is very important to the public's physical health. It enables people to avoid foods they are allergic to or that don't agree with them. It better allows people to generally manage their diets and health.

As beneficial as the food labeling law is to public health, many food companies didn't voluntarily label such information until the law was passed. In other words, until the food labeling law was actually passed, many companies gave higher regard to maximum profit than to their consumers' health. But, once it passed, those same consumers were given the opportunity to reward the healthier-food providers with their business at the expense of manufacturers whose products catered less to our health and more to our taste buds.

I propose to simply copy the concept of food labeling to DE&I, so that consumers can reward inclusive organizations with their business and penalize excluding organizations. In other words, we're asking companies to add a DE&I label on a prominent place on their homepage that gives the correct breakdown of their employee diversity, a label that reflects their real DE&I actions and outcomes, rather than their rhetoric.

Our collective consumer power will do the rest, rewarding brands with true workforce diversity and giving their products preference over excluding brands. In this way, we'll harness the power of a competitive free-market economy to do the work for us, by changing the current corporate competition from the companies who talk the best DE&I talk, to those that boast the best DE&I outcomes on their diversity labels. It should be as basic as food manufacturers labeling the ingredients of their food. And just as we shouldn't buy foods from brands that hide what they consist of, we shouldn't buy from brands that hide who their workforce does (and doesn't) consist of. We, the consumers, have that power, and it's time we wielded it.

#RESERVEEMPLOYMENT
(FOR THE OPPORTUNITY DEPRIVED)

On the one hand, it can be argued that the concept of reserved employment is already accepted and acted upon. Indeed, many large companies have reserved certain jobs for Black people or women in order to forward their diversity efforts, a trend that has intensified since #BlackLivesMatter and #MeToo movements. In a world in which the global Fortune 500 have more senior executives named John than women, such efforts are not only expected but much needed by large brands from a public relations point of view.[1]

These efforts serve to prove that large companies are very sensitive to public sentiment regarding equality, diversity, and inclusion, and they wish to stave off public criticism by demonstrating their efforts to become more inclusive. However, to my mind, such efforts fall very far from upholding their real social responsibilities. They are token inclusion efforts that often serve as a smokescreen, and they are a deviation from their real social responsibilities as large employers. In essence, they are trying to placate public sentiment by reserving a handful of high-profile jobs for extremely talented people who happen to be Black, with a disability, or female.

The concept of Reserved Employment for the Opportunity Deprived (REOD) that I wish to promote refers to employment underdogs who are chronically unemployed and who often need potential employers to create nurturing workplace environments in order that they hold down a job successfully and for the long term. The larger and more successful the company is, the more it should challenge itself by employing people who are harder to keep (as we have previously discussed). The whole point of reserved employment is to bring into the job market those who are chronically out of it, precisely because they are more challenging to employ or because they need warmer and more caring work cultures.

To illustrate, lets briefly examine two reserved employment practices. Microsoft posted in August 2021 that it needed an "accessibility support specialist" to help make its products more accessible to various populations. I'm sure Microsoft would be happy to find a person with disabilities who's qualified for that specific job, and the company might even give some preference to a candidate with disabilities over others. However, the first line of the required qualifications for the job (out of many) was, "6+ years of working with assistive technologies. Examples: NVDA, JAWS, ZoomText, Dragon Naturally Speaking."[2]

Now I'm sure you would agree that anyone with these qualifications is obviously not chronically unemployed, and if suitable applicants with disabilities and with over six years' experience with these technologies can be found, they probably won't demand any extra effort from Microsoft at all, other than goodwill.

This kind of reserved employment approach is in effect saying the following: "We're looking for people with great qualifications, and we'll hire the best applicants we can find. However, if we can find someone good enough who is with a disability, Black, female, or from an ethnic minority, we'll come out looking inclusive and diverse so that's a bonus for us—two birds with one stone!"

In comparison, let's look at Lemon Tree Hotels' (LTHs') efforts with women acid survivors—women who have been horribly disfigured by acid attacks (often perpetrated by family members, husbands, or boyfriends). These women don't just carry horrible physical scars. The emotional trauma, the prolonged physical pain, coming to terms with the disfigurement, the shame—all these leave deep psychological scars on the victims that can at times run deeper and cause more suffering than the physical scars.

It's difficult to imagine the scope and depth of human suffering these victims needed to endure in order to recover. And if they manage to do so, they are immediately confronted with a new unbearable reality: their disfigurement has transformed them, in the eyes of many, into the monster that little children cringe away from in the street. Can you imagine what it must feel like to have people shudder at the sight of you, daily? It really is hard to think of a population more deserving of a chance, of acceptance, of human caring, of working alongside people who see them as people, humans and not as disfigured outcasts.

When Lemon Tree Hotels decided to employ acid victims, it knew that it was not just the physical scars that it would need to contend with. Lemon Tree Hotels didn't decide to take this path because it found a group of highly qualified and experienced veteran hotel workers from the industry who just happened to be acid survivors, and the company thought, "Great, two birds with one stone." No, the company decided to work with acid survivors because it believed that as one of the leading hotels chains in India, it was their social responsibility to the community and one of their core values. Working with previously unemployed acid victims requires employers to invest extensively in training, rehabilitation, and emotional support, as well as preparing existing teams to socially onboard the acid survivors with warmth, empathy, and care.

The difference between the two companies when it comes to DE&I is great indeed. Microsoft (with financial capabilities hundreds of times that of Lemon Tree Hotels, if not more) is willing to reserve a few jobs for exceptionally talented people who happen to be from diverse populations. In contrast, Lemon Tree Hotels looks for employees with no prior experience among the community's least employed populations—people whose success will require Lemon Tree to make special widespread effort. And the beneficiaries of these efforts compose fully 20 percent of their entire workforce.

If all large corporations reserve employment the way Microsoft does, many of the world's employment underdogs will remain unemployed. But if all large corporations reserve employment the way Lemon Tree Hotels does, the global workforce will become truly inclusive, and very few of our brothers and sisters will remain chronically unemployed.

Ask yourself these questions: If I had a choice (with all things being equal), where would I be happier and prouder to work? Where would I feel a deeper sense of purpose or even of honor? At a company that reserves employment the way Microsoft does, or at a company that does it with the breadth, depth, and commitment of Patu Keswani, Aradhana Lal, and Lemon Tree Hotels?

Reserved Employment for the Opportunity Deprived: Definition and Best Practices

The purpose of REOD is to bring into the workplace employee underdogs who have a hard time finding and keeping a job. As such, REOD efforts should adhere to the following standards:

> *Target populations:* There should be a positive correlation between the financial power of a company and the challenge and effort they put into their REOD policies. In other words, the larger the company, the more financially successful it is, the more they should challenge themselves to hire the chronically unemployed tough cases from the surrounding community.

> *Overall percentage:* There should be a positive correlation between the financial power of a company to the percentage of entry-level jobs they reserve for the opportunity deprived. In other words, the larger the company, the more financially successful it is, the higher the percentage of jobs they should reserve for the opportunity deprived.

> *Transparency—DE&I label:* Companies' homepages should include a DE&I label, which provides detailed information regarding their REOD practices. People should be able to tell at a glance which challenged populations they hire and what percent of their workforce is reserved for them.

Push from the Bottom

REOD is a *push-from-the-bottom strategy* to facilitate diversity and inclusion. We want to afford those left out of the job market real options to successfully get and keep a job.

But what about employee underdogs who are currently working but lack true equity (the E part of DE&I)? These are people who have the capability to perform more complex roles for higher pay, but because they are from marginalized populations—employee underdogs—they often find themselves overtaken by less capable but more mainstream applicants or coworkers. How do we afford underdogs not only equal opportunity but also equal chance of success and advancement?

People working in a company that practices REOD at decent levels (reserving at least 5 percent of entry-level jobs for the community's chronically unemployed) will live with diversity every day, and they will be called upon to participate in the company's diversity efforts (as we saw, true diversity efforts need to involve most employees in order to succeed).

In such workplace environments, it's difficult to hold on to prejudicial beliefs, as people are daily reminded that some very impressive people they work alongside are from disadvantaged populations. Watching employees with walkers turn up at work with a smile every day, do their job well, and support the other employees on the team changes people's perceptions. In effect, the whole company is constantly reminded that quality and talent are independent of genders, colors, disabilities, and beliefs. Thus, establishing equity in entry-level jobs will transform the culture, which will eventually trickle up and affect equity in senior-level jobs.

But we don't have to wait for companies to adopt REOD for entry-level positions to further corporations' equity efforts regarding more senior positions. Some startups, like Joonko, have risen to the challenge to help large corporations with precisely that.

When a company tries to diversify their workforce and reserves jobs for people from a diverse population, Native Americans, for example, many Native American applicants will send their résumés, but only one will be chosen. Joonko collects the résumés of those Native Americans who weren't chosen, so that other companies looking for Native Americans for similar jobs can have a large group to choose from and so that people who were turned down from one job can easily find other similar openings to apply for.

When DE&I labeling becomes a thing, and REOD becomes widely adopted, we will still need to address the current (emotionally cold) corporate culture and transition it to one of caring. This change is crucial for making the modern workplace accessible to people who need working environments of human warmth and caring in order to function well. It is also direly needed by many (perhaps most) of those currently working who suffer from various degrees of work-related emotional problems like anxiety, stress, and depression. This is the third and final target that corporations need to aim for if we wish to achieve social justice in the workplace.

#WORKPLACECARING:
ACHIEVING A CORPORATE
CULTURE OF CARING

Changing the culture of huge organizations is always a challenge. With companies spread out globally while employing many thousands of employees, where do you start? With whom? What do you do? How do you coordinate?

I believe that such a huge undertaking can be much simplified by promoting just two processes: labeling jobs that are emotionally hazardous as such, and making all managerial bonuses contingent on employee well-being (as well as DE&I outcomes).

Labeling Emotionally Hazardous Jobs

Some jobs like mining, logging, or firefighting are by definition physically dangerous and are considered hazardous. When employers have hazardous jobs, they are responsible to inform employees, train them, and protect them. Employers are also required to use color codes, posters, labels, or signs to warn employees of potential hazards in their work space.

The U.S. Department of Labor even has a definition of *hazard pay*: "Additional pay for performing hazardous duty or work involving physical hardship. Work duty that causes extreme physical discomfort and distress which is not adequately alleviated by protective devices and is deemed to impose a physical hardship."[3] Unfortunately, current laws do not require employers to pay extra for jobs that fall under the above definition of *hazardous*.

Extra pay or not, according to the Department of Labor, employers are responsible for their employees' safety and health, with no distinction made between physical and emotional health.[4] If employers need to use color codes, posters, labels, or signs to warn employees of potential physical hazards, they should also warn employees if a job has potential emotional hazards.

Emotional hazards can be an integral part of the job, as in the case of paramedics or senior corporate executives. Emotional hazards can also be culture related—for instance, a corporation's culture characterized by constant stress, little regard for work-life balance, and an expectation that people answer emails at night and on weekends. (As an aside here, Portugal in 2021 passed a law stating that employers who send work-related emails to their employees after 6 p.m. will be fined!). Lastly, jobs can be emotionally hazardous because of people, for instance, a boss who has anger management issues or who constantly stresses, belittles, and harasses subordinates.

It's time employers took care of their employees' emotional health as well as their physical health, and a good place to start is to give the same regard to emotional hazards that they give to physical ones. Jobs that entail emotional stress, anxiety, or a constant disregard for work-life balance should be publicly regarded as such and marked as potentially emotionally distressing.

Additionally, jobs labeled as intrinsically emotionally hazardous should come with increased availability to emotional health monitoring and treatment. Jobs that are emotionally hazardous because of corporate culture or domineering bosses should cause correctly motivated employers to immediately intervene in order to change the emotionally toxic culture and curtail (train or dismiss) the abusive manager.

But how do we get employers to become correctly motivated?

Top-Down Accountability: Managerial Bonuses Contingent on Employee Well-Being and DE&I Outcomes

Capitalistic societies have a very effective built-in carrot called "money." If in just one fiscal year, all senior executives in a corporation did not receive yearly bonuses because the corporation was far from meeting its DE&I targets, I would guess that, by hook or by crook, the following year would see an influx of many new employee underdogs.

In order to motivate those with the most power to oversee the needed changes, the managers who should be penalized the most for missing DE&I targets are the corporation's senior executives, the same people who gain the most when the corporation does financially well.

Similarly, if a manager's subordinates feel harassed, bullied, belittled, or totally uncared for, the manager's bonus should also be partially or fully withheld. Succeeding at your job while overworking everyone and making them miserable should not be rewarded. On the other hand, managers who care for their subordinates and create a warm work environment should be rewarded with full bonuses.

Granted, current managerial practices and training programs don't usually focus on managing by caring, and many managers probably feel they don't possess the necessary toolbox to adopt a caring managerial style and remain an effective manager. I'm sure, however, that corporate America could easily design training programs to assist managers in the transition to a warmer management style. Compared to other corporate initiatives, it wouldn't be very complicated or costly, and large companies could complete such training within a year or two—provided, of course, all the relevant decision makers and stakeholders are correctly motivated.

To summarize, corporate America needs to change three things. They need to become transparent and adopt diversity labeling. They need to reserve employment for employment underdogs, specifically those individuals from the community who are the most chronically unemployed. Finally, they need to label emotionally hazardous jobs and make managerial bonuses contingent on DE&I outcomes and employee well-being, especially among senior management to ensure top-down accountability.

HOW TO MOTIVATE CHANGE

Once we know what changes corporate America needs to make, we need to examine how to motivate what some might say are sweeping changes—especially since we're asking those in charge to take upon themselves an obligation that might, and probably will, negatively affect their own individual income.

Obviously, proving that DE&I creates a large financial upside to employers, as I did in Chapter 1, doesn't work. After all, the research and data I've provided are public knowledge and known to many directors, at least in part. HR departments are aware of the financial importance of employee engagement, purpose, and work-life balance. They read about it, write about it, and measure it. But despite the wide dissemination of this knowledge, most corporate cultures are as cold and uncaring as can be.

So how do we bring about enough pressure on employers to cause them to gradually adopt DE&I labeling, reserve employment for the opportunity deprived (REOD), and develop a corporate culture of caring? And do all this while endangering substantial portions of their personal compensation? Who are the vehicles of change? Who can drum up enough weight to actually tilt those heavy scales?

There is only one entity I can think of that wields that much power. The corporations' patrons, its customers . . . in other words, us. Because when you think about it—without us, there is no them.

If a large portion of a company's customers demand a certain change, like it or not, regardless of cost, the company will make that change. It's been proven before. Remember?

The New Coke

In 1981, Coca-Cola's senior executives launched Project Kansas, which was tasked with the goal of improving both the taste and sales of the original Coke. They invested four years, millions of dollars, and conducted 200,000 taste tests. In 1985, they held a huge press conference and launched the New Coke.

Within one month, sales were 8 percent higher than the previous year (in places where the product was launched), and the senior executives were happy. However, many customers were not.

They voiced their objections through calls and letters to the company (this was pre-internet). The company hotline received four times the number of daily calls than normal. And letters accusing Coke's executives with everything from intruding on tradition to selling out to the Yankees (southern states took the introduction of New Coke the hardest) poured in.

On July 11, 1985, just 79 days after New Coke's introduction, a return of the original formula was announced. A senator called the reversal a "meaningful moment in US history."[5] It was awarded "breaking news" status, and it was announced on a special break from regular programming. The whole affair afforded Coca-Cola embarrassment and financial loss.

In the late 1990s, Coca-Cola's marketing vice president at the time of the New Coke launch summed up the New Coke experience thus: "Yes, it infuriated the public, cost us a ton of money and lasted for only 77 days before we reintroduced Coca-Cola Classic. Still, New Coke was a success because it revitalized the brand and reattached the public to Coke."[6]

I contend that what, in fact, revitalized the brand was that it had listened to its customers strongly felt wishes. Probably not much more than 100,000 customers caused the best-known brand in the world to come to a tire-burning stop and negotiate a full 180-degree turn, while enduring humiliation and loss. All within less than three months.

Don't doubt for a minute the power of your business and the clout you hold as a consumer. It can overcome even the biggest of corporate giants—as long as enough voices are raised and as long as they demand the same changes.

Earlier in this book, I detailed what changes corporate America should undergo. We are the vehicles of that change, the customers and employees who fuel these companies with our labor and purchases. What follows is what each of us should do and how things could transpire if enough of us choose to act.

Recruit an Army for Bottom-Up Change

I would argue that the real vehicles of change should be, can be, and, I believe, will be motivated individuals. It will start with a few family members of employee underdogs and sufferers of uncaring corporate cultures. Those few will ignite a spark that will ripple out to other family members of excluded employee underdogs, and they will ripple the effects to other loved ones who have had enough of corporate hypocrisy regarding DE&I.

So many people are either excluded, disadvantaged, or just work-related unhappy that the ripple effect started by few will be enlarged by many and will eventually touch all. You may ask, "Why haven't we objected to the lack of inclusion before? Why haven't we raised our collective voices regarding our emotional treatment at work until now?"

The answer is that we have been psychologically conditioned to view ourselves as inconsequential in a large world inhabited by extremely large and powerful entities, such as governments and giant global corporations. It seems fanciful to us to believe that an individual or small group of individuals can really have an impact, really create large-scale change. It seems and feels like a lost cause, and all because of the psychological conditioning we have undergone for generations.

Understand Collective Learned Helplessness

In all democracies, many people don't vote because they often don't believe that their vote will make a difference. (The last presidential election in the United States in which the voting turnout surpassed 80 percent was in 1876, and turnout has been in a decline since then. In the past 50 years, voting turnout has been mostly between 50 and 60 percent.)

It's not that we don't want change. Most of us really do, and most of us are willing to put in effort to bring about change. Alas, it's our lack of belief that our own personal endeavors will have any real effect in bringing about various changes that mutes our voices and curtails our actions.

In this regard, many of us have acquired *learned helplessness*, a psychological learned condition in which, after a few unsuccessful attempts at changing something, we adopt the view that we are incapable of changing it and helpless regarding it, and we stop trying. Even when circumstances change and success is then possible, people with learned helplessness won't resume their attempts to bring about the change they wanted. In effect, their overwhelming feelings of helplessness trick them into believing that they don't have the capacity to succeed and there is no point in further attempts, even when the objective situation would reward any further attempts with success.

But we don't need everyone to get over their "learned DE&I helplessness" simultaneously; things don't always start that way. Even the biggest social changes can be started by very few.

THE POWER OF THE FEW

The truth is that even a handful of individuals can light a spark that galvanizes masses, and small groups of individuals can bring about profound change on a national level. It's happened many times before, and it's usually been fueled by the power of love and caring, the same power that can break the conditioning of psychological learned helplessness.

Mothers Against Drunk Driving

The organization Mothers Against Drunk Driving (MADD) was founded in 1980 by Candace Lightner after her 13-year-old daughter was killed by a drunk driver. Channeling her pain into purpose, Candace Lightner was joined by Cindi Lamb and other grieving mothers, and a mere six months after founding MADD, their first national press conference was held in Washington, DC. Within two years, MADD's efforts were rewarded when President Ronald Reagan appointed the first commission on drunk driving, with MADD as a member.

That same year, the Alcohol Traffic Safety Law was passed, which provided various drunk driving countermeasures. The momentum for change continued. By 1988, every state had raised the legal age of drinking to 21. By 2013, the number of Americans killed by drunk driving had been cut by 55 percent since MADD's founding in 1980.

In a similar fashion, parental love—which as MADD proved is a huge motivator—has a key role to play in changing the current DE&I practices of corporate America.

Community for Creative Non-Violence

The Community for Creative Non-Violence (CCNV) was founded by J. Edward Guinan in 1970. CCNV is a Washington, DC–based charity that provides services to the poor and homeless, including food, shelter, clothing, medical care, case management, education, and art programs.[7]

In 1973, CCNV was joined by activist Mitch Snyder, and together they pressured the District of Columbia, as well as various religious institutions, to allow homeless people a safe place to sleep at night (inside the religious and public institutions themselves). They protested, held public funerals for homeless people who had frozen to death on DC streets, and fasted. They were extremely influential in creating various shelters for the homeless in Washington, DC, and they made homelessness a national and international public interest issue.

Housing First

Mitch Snyder and the CCNV's efforts galvanized the Housing First policy, which entails offering permanent housing as quickly as possible to homeless people, followed by other supportive services. Begun in 1988 to address the needs of homeless families with children in Los Angeles, California, Housing First grew in popularity in the following decades, and it became the primary government policy for addressing homelessness in the United States and many other countries. The US Congress in 1999 directed that the Department of Housing and Urban Development (HUD) spend 30 percent of its funding on the Housing First method.[8]

The implementation of Housing First has had a huge impact. When working with homeless families and young adults, it has been shown to increase clients' enrollment in public assistance benefits programs and to decrease involvement in the child welfare system. Most notably, very few return to homelessness.[9]

Furthermore, in August 2007, HUD reported that the number of chronically homeless individuals living on the streets or in shelters dropped by an unprecedented 30 percent, from 175,914 people in 2005 to 123,833 in 2007. This was credited in part to the Housing First approach.

In summation, the actions of a few committed people took homelessness from a fringe problem many were unaware of and unengaged with, placed it on the national stage, and succeeded in influencing and changing policies and funding on a national level. Their actions undoubtedly saved many lives and improved the living conditions of countless others.

The Four Mothers

The Four Mothers was an Israeli social protest movement founded in 1997 by four mothers of soldiers in the Israel Defense Forces (IDF) whose sons were serving (and dying) in the south of Lebanon for many years.

Background

In 1982, Israel invaded Lebanon in order to secure an end to the frequent bombardments of northern Israeli towns by Palestinian insurgents operating out of the south of Lebanon. Following three years of fighting, in 1985 Israel declared the south of Lebanon a "security zone," and they remained deployed there together with Lebanese Christian Militias, in order to protect Israel's northern border from further bombardments.

Over the years, the IDF suffered many casualties. In 1997, 73 young Israeli soldiers were killed in a helicopter crash en route to the security zone. Four mothers of IDF soldiers from the north of Israel decided to publicly call for a unilateral withdrawal of all IDF forces from southern Lebanon. It was an unpopular public view at the time, and it was considered unpatriotic to call for a withdrawal while soldiers were still embedded in the security zone and involved in daily clashes. The Four Mothers were accused of weakening the resolve of those who needed it to fight, survive, and protect the northern border.

The Israeli government had long contended publicly that the deployment wasn't permanent and that Israel would withdraw when circumstances permitted. That being said, until that time, it was considered a show of civic weakness to publicly voice concern over the lives of deployed soldiers. Israelis were expected to demonstrate stoic reserve in the face of casualties so that neighboring enemies (Israel is not widely popular in the region) could not exploit the cracks of civic weakness by inflicting even more casualties. Plus, it was considered unpatriotic to say anything that might cause Israeli soldiers to become demoralized and lose heart in the conflict.

The Four Mothers movement sparked loud and angry social controversy, and at first, its members were extremely unpopular with mainstream public opinion. The leaders were belittled because they were women, and they were accused of violating the values of Israeli culture. Their plea to maternal feelings often met with loud objections by female politicians and bereaved mothers who accused the movement of becoming a danger to Israeli society. An influential army colonel publicly referred to the Four Mothers movement as the "four rags." But while the four founders had never been in the public spotlight before and faced widespread public criticism, they stood fast.

They were fueled by their mission to prevent their sons (or any other IDF soldiers) from losing their lives on foreign soil in an unending and (in their view) unnecessary deployment. As unpopular as it was initially, they started public demonstrations in the summer of 1997, and their numbers swiftly grew. Their demonstrations spread to all of Israel and began to include other people besides mothers.

Loving and concerned parents, raising their collective voices for the welfare of their children, are a force to be reckoned with, and within a mere three years, the four Israeli mothers—previously unknown in the public sphere—had successfully coerced the Israeli government to conduct a full and complete withdrawal from southern Lebanon (completed by May 2000). Following the retreat, with their goals achieved, they fully disbanded the movement.

The Powerful Spark That Set the Movement in Motion

During those three years, especially at the beginning, the four founding mothers endured not only harsh public criticism but also many nasty personal attacks from friends, neighbors, politicians, generals, and some members of the press. They held their ground with surprising resilience and fortitude.

The four were remarkably driven and motivated. Understandably, people were curious regarding what had inspired them and hardened their resolve. Many years later, in an interview, they revealed that they were set off by a spark that they described as a huge slap in the face, a ringing blow that shocked them to their cores and directly galvanized them to form the movement and to persist in the face of nonstop criticism.

The spark was an editorial opinion, written for a small news outlet with just a few thousand readers, and it devastated them. It was subtitled, "Stop Crying After (Your Sons Die), You Did Nothing to Prevent It (Their Deaths)," written by Eran Shahar, a young journalist who had fought in Lebanon 15 years previously. Eran's editorial bluntly blamed Israeli mothers of IDF soldiers for abandoning their maternal instincts; for shamefully forgoing the lives of their sons; and sacrificing generation after generation of young Israelis on the altar of unnecessary military campaigns.

When I interviewed Eran about the affair, I was interested to discover how shocked he was that these Four Mothers had managed to succeed in their mission.

"They were just . . . four mothers," he explained. "Not especially charismatic, they didn't even know each other well. None of them were especially good orators, they had no personal funds, no high-ranking friends. They basically had nothing going for them. If initially you would have asked me what their chances of success were, I would honestly say—none."

To me the Four Mothers' story is the epitome of how a handful of people can change the lives of millions of other people. It teaches us how the few can cause the many to see a grievance that they were previously oblivious to, how the few can galvanize the many to object to this grievance and act together to change it. If the struggle is just enough, if it touches enough people, if it is relevant and affects enough people, then even just a handful of regular, unknown individuals can start us on a journey that will, at its culmination and fulfillment, enrich all our lives. We don't actually need a large force to achieve these kinds of victories. But it's encouraging to realize that we happen to have an army on our side. And it's enormous!

THE SIZE OF OUR ARMY

In 2019, the U.S. Census Bureau estimated that Hispanic and Latino (of any race) composed 18.5 percent of the population; Black or African Americans, 13.4 percent; and Asians, 5.9 percent. People with disabilities compose 10 to 15 percent of all groups. Combine these four groups and you get close to 50 percent of the population. Add loved ones and family, and the number rises to well over 50 percent of the population.

If we really want change, we definitely have the numbers on our side. The only question is, how should we leverage this advantage?

The Hashtag Revolution

We can use the same principles that enabled #MeToo and #Black-LivesMatter to have a huge ripple effect. According to Wikipedia: "The phrase 'Me too' was tweeted by Alyssa Milano around noon on October 15, 2017, and had been used more than 200,000 times by the end of the day, and tweeted more than 500,000 times by the end of the next day. On Facebook, the hashtag was used by more than 4.7 million people in 12 million posts during the first 24 hours. The platform reported that 45 percent of users in the United States had a friend who had posted using the term."[10]

Again, according to Wikipedia: "In 2014, the American Dialect Society chose #BlackLivesMatter as their word of the year. From July 2013 through May 1, 2018, the hashtag '#BlackLivesMatter' had been tweeted an average of 17,002 times per day. On May 28, 2020, there were nearly 8.8 million tweets with the hashtag, and the average had increased to 3.7 million a day."[11]

Join the Hashtag Revolution:
Three Hashtags, 30 Seconds a Day

We have a huge army, we have a voice via social media, and we can use both to create profound change. If you really believe in equality, diversity, and inclusion. If you believe the modern workplace should transform into one of caring and human warmth. If you believe your employer should strive to stop all instances of bullying, harassment, and belittling. If you want to end your work-related anxiety, stress, or depression. If you want your children to work in places that treat them with equity, dignity, and respect. If you want a future in which everyone who wants to work can find a job that will suit their capabilities, strengths, and frailties. If you want the modern workplace to represent the true diversity of our communities. If you want any of these things, all you need to do is invest 30 seconds of your time, per day, 10 seconds per hashtag.

Use the three hashtags—#DiversityLabels, #ReserveEmployment, and #WorkplaceCaring—once a day in your social media. You can do it while riding on public transportation, while sipping your morning coffee, or while sitting on the toilet. You can post just the hashtags, you can mention them in a sentence, you can use them as comments on other people's posts. #BlackLivesMatter averaged 3.7 million posts a day, and Black people compose 13.4 percent of the US population. Employee underdogs and loved ones compose four times that number of people.

Use your social voice to promote your values and the need for global equality. Invest 30 seconds of your time, every day, in order to promote these three hashtags from the comfort of your own home. It's a fight for equality, for the overlooked, and your own personal, work-related emotional health.

We are legion, our cause is just, and it's time to join the 30-seconds-a-day hashtag revolution for true equality. Your one voice, each individual action, is a mere ripple in the pond. But together, eventually, perhaps quickly, we can create a wave large enough to drown out the injustice we have levied on our marginalized brothers and sisters for too long. The time for change is now, and it's a change fueled by our unspoken commitment to our family and friends and by our love.

We can all win, as long as we win with *all* the underdogs.

Afterword

How and Why I Started This Journey

I believe that change, the message this book wishes to promote, is entirely more important than the messenger: myself. And as far as the message goes, the book is complete.

I wrote the following for those interested in my personal motivations:

> When crushing life events suddenly tear you from your path propelling you toward perpetual darkness, it is sometimes possible to influence your own trajectory, so that you can eventually end up flying even closer to the light. —G. W.

I was born optimistic. Some people tend to see mainly negatives. I can see negatives too, but for me, the negatives fade and are continuously outshined by the positives. Even when things go badly or look grim, I naturally find myself noting the negatives but actively being drawn to and listing the positives and opportunities.

YOU HAVE AN INCURABLE DISEASE

When I turned 40, my wife insisted I go for a physical (I hadn't had one in years). I had a full checkup and promptly forgot about it. Three days later the doctor called and asked me to come in. I was feeling fine, so I wasn't sure what to expect. I sat down in the doctor's office with my wife, expecting a "your cholesterol is a bit high" or a "you've put on 10 pounds in the past few years" sort of chat.

The doctor went straight to the point. In a blunt and emotionless manner, he said, "You have what I believe to be non-Hodgkin's lymphoma. It's well advanced, I can feel lumps in your neck, armpits, groin, . . . and this specific kind . . . it's incurable. I'm sorry."

"At some point," he continued slowly, "your cancer will either be unresponsive to treatments, or it will mutate to a much more violent cancer."

I leaned over and hugged my wife's shaking body as the doctor's words slowly sank in. Mutate? Unresponsive?

"Doctor, how long do I have?" I managed to ask.

"It varies between months to maybe even a few years," he answered. "Your cancer is very widespread; it could be sooner. You need to prepare."

When I got home, I faced the horrible task many cancer newbies confront: informing everyone I cared about in the world that I was diagnosed with terminal cancer—my identical twin brother, my mother, other family members, friends. It was the darkest task imaginable. There was no hope to offer them, no words of solace or comfort. Afterward, I felt cold, weak, and utterly helpless.

I finished that horrendous task and got on with the business of dying. The next few weeks were a whirlwind of hospitals, tests, doctors, and opinions. I was cold all the time, the kind of cold you feel when you're very, very scared.

My mind was fully consumed with the horrific implications of dying. My emotional range shrank to feelings of fear, sadness, and grief. I had an incurable disease, and time was truly my most precious asset. Yet I was wasting it, days and weeks of it, engulfed in misery, unable to shake the horror of my situation, beaten and emotionally powerless.

FIGHTING BACK

Then one morning, I woke up with a different feeling, one so powerful it rocked me to the core. Instead of the cold, debilitating fist of fear I constantly felt in my stomach, I felt hot inside. In fact, I was burning. It wasn't the flush-faced burning of a fever. It came from my gut, where the constant cold used to emanate from. Overnight, my fear had been replaced with a feeling just as strong and overpowering, but different. Rage.

Something deep within me was screaming, "Enough!" I had had it with dying, absolutely had it! I realized I wasn't feeling miserable or sad or scared anymore. I was so angry, there wasn't room for any other emotion. I was furious—at my doctors, who had left me no hope at a time when medical breakthroughs came at a breathtaking pace, at fate, life, the world.

But I was, first and foremost, furious at myself. Furious for wasting precious time, livid that I had so totally succumbed to fear and helplessness that I had turned my back so quickly on who I really was as a person, on who I had been all my adult life. I had given up! Tapped out! Without a fight! Me! I was no longer shaking from fear. I was shaking from rage, deep intense rage.

It was as though hope knocked at my door—from the inside.

That morning, lying in bed, I decided to fight back, to literally fight for my life, to focus all my thoughts, emotions, and efforts on what I *could* do. And I knew that I had to start my wars in the only arena in which I could eventually gain full control—my mind. I decided to be the first person who refused to die from the kind of cancer

I had. I refused to hand my doctors the right of governance over when I live and when I die. Enough! I was going to get control back.

I realized there were two things I could influence greatly. First, my physical state. Even with cancer, I could and would greatly improve my general conditioning, stamina, nutrition, and strength. Second, my emotional state. I needed to teach myself how to live a long, happy, and meaningful life, albeit with cancer as a constant background companion, but free of fear and constant thoughts of doom.

Strengthening My Body

Recognizing that my body faced huge challenges and that I was out of shape, I decided to do something that, to me, represented the pinnacle of human health and conditioning—run a half marathon, 13 miles (and schlepp every tumor in my body along with me).

I started running every day. At first, all I could manage was a mile or two before cramps and retching kicked in and caused me to stop. But I kept going, increasing my distance a little every day. In a few weeks, I was running cramp and nausea free.

I had no talent for distance running, but what I lacked in ability I made up for in persistence and perseverance. When needed, I came up with various tricks and schemes to keep myself motivated and not to miss runs, even when the weather was terrible or I felt too tired. I would lie to myself, pretending that completing the allotted mileage of the day's run would completely heal me. Or I would use guilt, reminding myself how upset I was when I thought there was nothing I could do to actively fight back. So I should be grateful that I discovered that I can fight back with something so easy to do, such as a little run.

My ultimate motivator was my family. I would envision one of them standing off to the side cheering me on, shouting how proud they are of me, encouraging me to keep going, to fight, to keep doing everything I could to live. I used every drop of that love to keep myself motivated daily. Love was—and still is—the most powerful weapon in my arsenal.

Strengthening My Mind

To strengthen my mind and my emotional well-being, I turned to my values and beliefs, as so many others do at such times. I have always believed that this is the only shot we have at life, so we should each try to leave the "room" tidier when we "check out" than it was when we "checked in," so to speak. I wanted my life to make a difference, so I started looking for a wrong I could right. I wanted it to be a big one.

As is sometimes the case, when one begins a search for purpose with a truly open mind, the answer often presents itself. Soon thereafter, I had coffee with a quadriplegic friend who was the head of a foundation that focused on improving accessibility for people with disabilities.

As we discussed his recent endeavors, he happened to mention the high rates of unemployment among people with severe disabilities. At first, I thought those numbers made sense. If people had such severe disabilities that warranted a full disability pension, they really couldn't work.

But then I became curious. I realized there was something that did not make any kind of sense at all. Most people I knew worked in offices, at computer stations. My friend was in a wheelchair, but he was perfectly able to run a foundation. So why couldn't other people in wheelchairs work at computer stations too? Why do they have such high unemployment rates?

And it wasn't just people who were wheelchair bound. For example, most people who were legally blind had some sight left, and with special software that enlarges text, they could function quite well— as evidenced by their use of computers and cell phones. So why were they so drastically unemployed?

Why was this state of affairs equally dismal among those whose disabilities were emotional and psychological? Indeed, a third of those receiving disability pensions were classified as having an emotional disability. Most of them were compliant with their medication and were generally stable. So why were so many of them not working?

I began meeting with people who had a variety of severe disabilities, and I mapped out the different reasons that might explain their chronic unemployment. Ironically, during that time, my own medical condition garnered me the dubious classification of being considered as having 100 percent disability myself, at least as far as the government was concerned. I had officially become part of the group I was studying, even though the only limitation imposed on my functioning was my looming expiration date.

However, I was keenly aware of the huge difference between my circumstances and those of the people I was studying. Other than my abbreviated life expectancy, I suffered none of the societal ills they dealt with on a daily basis—isolation and chronic poverty. Living in a constant financial battle for survival causes huge ongoing stress, depression, and anxiety.

FINDING MY PATH

My new life mission was beginning to form.

Obviously, I could not find remedies for the disabilities themselves, but what if I could do something about the employment issues of people with disabilities? Getting people with disabilities jobs would not only help them financially, it could potentially take care of the other two unnecessary banes in their lives—poverty and isolation.

Yes, I had my cancer to fight, but there was a huge discrepancy between the lifespan my doctors projected for me and the lifespan I projected for myself. I figured I would have time to take on my new mission.

Plus, I felt a strong kind of cosmic kinship with people who have disabilities. While I was attempting to break free of the life expectancy shackles imposed on me by my condition and the limitations of my doctors, people with disabilities need to break free of the employment shackles imposed on them by society's lack of knowledge regarding disability and employment.

I was fortunate enough to have the necessary background to wage this battle. I had an undergraduate degree in special education and a PhD in psychology. Further, I had extensive training in posttraumatic stress disorder (PTSD), and I had been working as an organizational psychologist for years. I was certain I could make a difference.

My future course was set. I would run a half marathon and figure out why people with disabilities have such high rates of unemployment. I called it Plan A.

PLAN A TAKES OFF

I spent the next year conducting research, interviewing people with disabilities, employers, social services professionals, and other experts in the field. I mapped out all the reasons so many people with disabilities don't work. I identified the challenges and the obstacles, and I began formulating possible solutions.

During this time, I visited the hospital a few times a month, where I underwent a variety of tests. I used these visits to strengthen my control over negative what-if thoughts. What if it's spread even more? What if my bloodwork is poor? What if I need chemo or a bone marrow transplant? What if nothing works? I knew I couldn't keep such thoughts completely out of my consciousness. But I resolved never to let them linger more than a second or two. It was an active battle, not a passive one. The minute a what-if negative thought entered my brain, I concentrated on envisioning something positive.

Throughout this process, I continued to run. Two years after I was diagnosed, I completed a half marathon. Crossing the finish line, I was so exhausted, I could barely stand up. I barely avoided throwing up on my exuberant daughters. But despite the exhaustion and nausea, I felt a huge sense of accomplishment.

I had completed the running half of Plan A. And I was also making progress on the disabilities and unemployment front. I felt like I had regained control of my life.

UPPING THE ANTE

The following week, I found out that my doctor was a little less thrilled with my accomplishments. It seemed that my cancer was determined not to give in quietly.

"You have a tumor in your left lung," my doctor informed me at my regular bimonthly checkup.

"No, I don't," I said.

She sighed and looked up from the chart she was looking at. "You do. It's right there," she said holding up the x-ray to the light and indicating a spot on my left lung.

"Not a tumor," I said. "I just ran a half marathon a few days ago," I pointed out. "You don't run half marathons with a tumor in your lung."

I wasn't being difficult. I really felt fine and in the best shape of my life. Turned out that I was right—subsequent tests showed that indeed there was no cancer in my lungs. It was an x-ray glitch. But it did get me thinking.

"You know," I said to my wife that evening, "I should really up the ante, so to speak."

"What do you mean?" she inquired.

"I've run a half marathon, I've figured out why people with disabilities are out of work, and still the cancer lingers. I need to ascertain my dominance," I said.

"Exactly how?" she pressed.

"I guess I'm going to go with what's been working for the past two years—running and people with disabilities. I want to run a full marathon. And I want to change the current reality where so many people with disabilities are out of work," I replied.

PLAN B TAKES OFF

Plan B was simple to define but a little tougher to execute. Run a full marathon and fix disability and unemployment—globally . . .

Over the next four years, I developed a unique managerial model that addressed all the issues and obstacles that my research showed were responsible for keeping many people with disabilities out of a job.

My hope was that my model would provide a blueprint for businesses to hire large groups of people with severe disabilities, chronically unemployed people, and show them how to create a workplace where these people can achieve regular productivity and earn regular wages in free-market conditions.

I believed I could prove that when people with severe disabilities were given the conditions they required and were managed in a manner that addressed their needs, they could attain a level of functioning in the workplace that equaled that of those who were able-bodied. And if I could do that, I could demonstrate that the chronic unemployment of people with severe disabilities was not due to their disability but to employers (and society at large) not understanding or addressing their true needs.

PLAN A GETS BIGGER

Once I started researching employment and disability, I quickly learned that there were many other underemployed groups: single parents, Arab Israeli women, ex-cons, people over 60, and others. I learned that employment underdogs made up a large group of the marginalized, different, and nonmainstream people and that the group included even people going through temporary confidence and self-efficacy issues.

I realized that I was building a model that could serve the needs of all employment underdogs. Indeed, we found over time that our model (I called it Links) was equally effective at identifying and nurturing potential among all sorts of employment underdog populations.

Sadly, the world can be a cynical place. In order to open the gates of employment to all groups of employment underdogs, I needed my model to succeed with those considered the most challenging to employ: people with severe disabilities. So I decided to focus my initial efforts on that group, with the thought that their success held the keys that could open employment doors for all other underdog groups.

Once the managerial model was complete, I searched for a company that would be willing to give people with severe disabilities a chance by using Links in its entirety—for screening, onboarding, training, and ongoing management. I leveraged personal and professional connections to set up meetings with CEOs from many companies, and I presented my pitch. They all turned me down, firmly.

As one of them put it, "It's a great idea, I'll give you that. But all it takes is one guy in a wheelchair outside our offices with a banner saying, 'I was fired because I have a disability,' and our brand and reputation would be in deep trouble. We just can't take that risk."

After more than a year of rejections, I was running out of options. Not one large company I had talked to was willing to hire people with severe disabilities. They didn't want the risk, they lacked bandwidth and commitment, and they were too busy with struggles of their own to invest in the struggles of others.

I began to confront the reality that if I wanted to demonstrate the effectiveness of Links, I would have to do it myself. *I* would have to be the employer. Like it or not, I would have to start and run my own company.

Given that I had to go it alone and my life expectancy was already in the red, so to speak, and given that I would have to invest my family's modest savings in the enterprise, I wanted to make sure I had my wife's blessing. We discussed it for hours, but ultimately, my wife reminded me that when we got married, we both had agreed to live our lives prioritizing experiences over material things. "And this definitely looks like it's going to be an experience," she said wryly.

A TERRIBLE IDEA

As my running improved, I decided to tell my doctor at one of my bimonthly checkups about my intention to run a full marathon.

"That's a terrible idea! Running for three hours straight is terribly taxing to the body," my doctor said.

"Well, that's OK then because I plan to take my time and go much more slowly, more like four or five hours running for me," I interjected sheepishly.

"I'm not joking! You have widespread stage four lymphoma, your immune system is compromised, and your body will be even more compromised after such a grueling ordeal," she said, giving me her "I'm dead serious" look.

Two weeks later, when I entered my doctor's office, there were three other doctors sitting there. She had called in backup.

"Your CT results are in," she said. "Unfortunately, they show five large tumors, all over two inches in size. The standard for starting chemo is three smaller tumors. It's progressed, and we need to start."

I waited for the dreaded fist of cold to sink in, and gave it a few more seconds . . . nothing. I examined my feelings just to make sure. Nope. I wasn't scared, upset, or even angry. I was surprised to discover that I was actually feeling very confident.

"You have to stop this marathon nonsense, and we need to start chemotherapy," one of the guest doctors said. "It's been a few years now, and you've put off treatment for as long as possible," said another.

"It's time," added the third.

Please understand, I was on good terms with these doctors. I knew they were there because they cared and wished the best for me. The thing is, they had limited experience (none actually) with terminal patients wanting to run marathons.

"Actually, it isn't time," I replied to all four doctors.

I had run 27 kilometers in training two days earlier. I realized that the scan showed tumor growth, but I knew I was getting stronger and healthier.

"I couldn't do 27 kilometers—in three hours" (I couldn't help the brag) "if I were getting worse."

Then I asked the million-dollar question.

"Will chemo prolong my life? As you all know, medical research says it won't, but I believe that running might. I truly appreciate your advice, but I'm going with 'no to chemo' at this time and 'yes to marathon.'"

It was double decision time: Go against the advice of all the experts and foundation leaders and pour all our savings into a one-of-a-kind experimental business no one thinks will succeed? At the same time, finish training and run the full marathon when all my doctors thought I should be in the hospital undergoing harsh chemotherapy and biological therapy. At that point, for me, it was a no-brainer—I followed my heart.

VICTORY

A year later, I ran the Athens Classical (uphill) Marathon, which ends inside the 2,000-year-old marble stadium in Athens. It was glorious.

My wife waited for me in the stands. I was so elated, I was a complete emotional mess and cried. Twice. The first time, as I crossed the finish line and I realized what I had accomplished, I burst into tears, engulfed in feelings of joy, life, health, and four and a half hours' worth of endorphins. The second time was when my wife informed me that because the race was still being run, we would have to walk for three kilometers uphill to get back to the hotel.

I kept following my heart. In 2008, seven years after I was diagnosed with terminal cancer and two years past my original "max expiration date," we launched Call Yachol (CY), the free-market, for-profit outsource call center that I discussed at length in Chapter 3.

In Hebrew, *Call Yachol* means "able to do anything." We thought the name apt. We conceived CY as a social business, and our hope was that CY would serve as a showcase—a proof of concept that would demonstrate that people with severe disabilities could achieve regular productivity in a free-market business for regular free-market wages. The call center would be staffed, managed, and operated entirely at first by people with severe disabilities.

CY TAKES OFF

We chose a call center because it is the ideal business to demonstrate employee productivity. In call centers, everything and everyone is measured electronically (for example, calls per hour and sales per hour), so it is the ideal platform for proving that a team of people with severe disabilities can measure up to other teams (of employees without disabilities) doing the same work—a true apples-to-apples comparison.

If we succeeded, it would change the perceptions and beliefs of employers and policy makers, as well as the ingrained feeling of many employment underdogs who had lost all hope of joining the workforce and becoming contributing members of society.

More importantly, the real-life benefits to our employees would be huge. They would be able to double or triple their incomes and lift themselves out of poverty. Some would finally leave the prison of their homes and spend their days among their coworkers and become better integrated into their communities. Those accomplishments would have a profound impact on their psychological quality of life: their self-esteem, their happiness, their family relationships, their sense of agency and efficacy. And perhaps, just perhaps, it might even serve to reverse some of the devastating impact that years of social rejection and social trauma had wrought.

During our first year of operations, we screened and trained three teams of call-center agents with a wide range of disabilities: People with amputations, people who use wheelchairs, people who were legally blind, or with full hearing loss (with cochlear implants), people with cerebral palsy and various other debilitating chronic conditions or injuries, as well as those with emotional disabilities. It typically took twice as long, but the majority of our inaugural class was able to achieve regular productivity and measure up to groups doing the same work in other call centers. We believed that the bigger investment in training would yield even bigger returns because of higher employee engagement and significantly reduced employee attrition.

Like most startups, we were very lean. We found early on that we needed someone who could take on a wide variety of functions, from recruitment to procurement to liaison with governmental agencies and other tasks. The only person I knew who was that generally competent was my wife, Efi. So a few months after opening our doors, my wife walked through them and joined me.

THE TRIUMPH OF PLAN B

It's been 14 years since then, and more than 20 years since I was initially diagnosed with terminal cancer—and so much has happened.

I ran three more marathons, and I was planning on running my fifth one, but life decided to intervene. After 12 years of an intense, emotional, roller-coaster relationship, it was apparent that one of us was unsatisfied with our mutual situation and wanted more than the other was willing to give. I guess that in many long-term relationships, one party grows or evolves faster than the other, and that discrepancy can cause a rift. Such was the case for us, and I realized that it was finally time to break up, to go our separate ways. I had always felt that we had a firm understanding between us, that our relationship could sustain the status quo, the delicate but lasting balance we had found, but it was not to be.

Joyfully for all of us, in the summer of 2013, my cancer and I decided to part ways. My doctors informed me that either my cancer had mutated into a more aggressive type, or a new cancer had decided to join the fray. I didn't even bother to undergo a biopsy in order to determine which of the two it was—as far as I was concerned, my cancer(s) and I were going our separate ways.

A year of (supposedly) harsh chemo, surgery, and biological treatments ensued. I was warned that my chemo regime was quite harsh and punitive and could create a long list of additional problems for my body along the way. I was also told that, in my case, hopes of a full remission were not realistic due to the type of cancer I had and the many years I had lived with it residing in my body.

Of course, I saw things differently. And happily, I was proven right.

I kept running throughout the year, taking only two months off toward the end. In fact, my wife's nausea during pregnancies was worse than I experienced during chemo. I generally felt OK. I kept on working, enjoyed not shaving, and found out that bald is a good look for me.

Halfway through chemo, a CT showed that no cancer resided in my body, and even though my official medical status still contends that I have incurable cancer, I don't plan on being the type of person who finds themselves returning to their ex after a few years without them.

As I mentioned at the beginning of this chapter, I was born happy and optimistic. And since I was diagnosed with cancer 20 years ago, the years that followed have been the happiest of my life.

I am surrounded with so much love, both at home and at work. I'm invigorated daily with our passion for making life easier for those less fortunate than we are. Until underdogs worldwide can equally gain employment, our lifework will relentlessly, but always happily, continue.

Notes

Introduction

1. United States Census Bureau, "Quick Facts: United States," https://www.census .gov/quickfacts/fact/table/US/PST045219.
2. Neil Bhutta, Andrew C. Chang, Lisa J. Dettling, and Joanne W. Hsu, "Dispari- ties in Wealth by Race and Ethnicity in the 2019 Survey of Consumer Finances," *FEDS Notes*, September 28, 2020, https://www.federalreserve.gov/econres /notes/feds-notes/disparities-in-wealth-by-race-and-ethnicity-in-the-2019 -survey-of-consumer-finances-20200928.htm.
3. World Economic Forum (WEF), *Insight Report: Global Gender Gap Report 2020* (Geneva, Switzerland: WEF, 2020), p. 5, https://www3.weforum.org/docs /WEF_GGGR_2020.pdf.
4. National Sexual Violence Resource Center (NSVRC), Statistics, https://www .nsvrc.org/statistics, accessed January 2022.
5. Deloitte, *Missing Pieces Report: The Board Diversity Census of Women and Mi- norities on Fortune 500 Boards*, 6th ed., https://www2.deloitte.com/us/en/pages /center-for-board-effectiveness/articles/missing-pieces-board-diversity-census -fortune-500-sixth-edition.html.
6. Max Woolf, "Workplace Bullying Is on the Rise (2021 Study)," October 3, 2021, https://www.myperfectresume.com/career-center/careers/basics/workplace -bullying-in-2021, accessed January 2022.
7. Amy Elisa Jackson, "New Study: 3 in 5 US Employees Have Witnessed or Expe- rienced Discrimination," Glassdoor, blog, July 22, 2020, https://www.glassdoor .com/blog/new-study-discrimination, accessed January 2022.
8. Dylan Love, "16 Examples of Steve Jobs Being a Huge Jerk," *Business Insider*, October 25, 2011, https://www.businessinsider.com/steve-jobs-jerk-2011-10, accessed January 2022.
9. "Eight Surprising Statistics About Interviews," Twin Group, Employment and Training, blog, March 14, 2018, https://www.twinemployment.com/blog/8 -surprising-statistics-about-interviews.
10. U.S. Department of Labor, Bureau of Labor Statistics, *Persons with a Disability: Labor Force Characteristics—2021*, https://www.bls.gov/news.release/pdf/disabl .pdf.

Chapter 1

1. Grace Donnelly, "Only 3% of Fortune 500 Companies Share Full Diversity Data," *Fortune*, June 7, 2017, https://fortune.com/2017/06/07/fortune-500-diversity.

2. *Brands Take a Stand: Edelman Earned Brand Global Report*, October 2018, p. 5, https://www.edelman.com/sites/g/files/aatuss191/files/2018-10/2018_Edelman _Earned_Brand_Global_Report.pdf.

3. Jim Harter and Annamarie Mann, "The Right Culture: Not Just About Employee Satisfaction," Gallop Workplace, blog, April 12, 2017, https://www.gallup .com/workplace/236366/right-culture-not-employee-satisfaction.aspx.

4. S. N. Downey, L. van der Werff, K. M. Thomas, and V. C. Plaut, "The Role of Diversity Practices and Inclusion in Promoting Trust and Employee Engagement," *Journal of Applied Social Psychology*, vol. 45, no. 1, 2015, pp. 35–44.

5. Lee Rowland and Oliver Scott Curry, "A Range of Kindness Activities Boosts Happiness," *Journal of Social Psychology*, vol. 159, no. 3, 2019, pp. 340–343.

6. Crystal Susan Wiedemann, Clemson University, *Purpose-Driven: Employee Engagement from a Human Flourishing Perspective*, dissertation, ProQuest Dissertations Publishing, May 2019, All Dissertations, 2349.

7. Elizabeth Renter, "Picture Improves for Homeowners," Nerdwallet, blog, April 25, 2018, https://www.nerdwallet.com/blog/mortgages/2018-homeownership-pulse.

8. Alan Murray, "America's CEOs Seek a New Purpose for the Corporation," *Fortune*, August 19, 2019, https://fortune.com/longform/business-roundtable -ceos-corporations-purpose.

9. "The Real Cost of Employee Turnover in 2021," Terra Staffing Group, blog, November 4, 2020, https://www.terrastaffinggroup.com/resources/blog/cost-of -employee-turnover/; Paula Morgan, "How to Avoid High Turnover Costs by Bringing Former Employees Back to Work," *Forbes*, May 24, 2021, https://www .forbes.com/sites/paulamorgan/2021/03/24/how-to-avoid-high-turnover-costs -by-bringing-former-employees-back-to-work/?sh=345bf4ea50a8, accessed January 2022; and Natasha Boddy, "The Real Cost of Losing a Star Performer," *Financial Review*, April 15, 2021, https://www.afr.com/work-and-careers/careers /the-real-cost-of-losing-a-star-performer-20200217-p541go.

10. Sundiatu Dixon-Fyle, Kevin Dolan, Vivian Hunt, and Sara Prince, *Diversity Wins: How Inclusion Matters*, McKinsey & Company, May 19, 2020, https:// www.mckinsey.com/featured-insights/diversity-and-inclusion/diversity-wins -how-inclusion-matters.

11. A study by the Varkey Foundation in collaboration with UNESCO: "A New Report Finds Fortune 500 Companies Commit a Fraction of CSR Spend on Education," UNESCO, https://en.unesco.org/news/new-report-finds-fortune -500-companies-commit-fraction-csr-spend-education.

12. Google leaders avoid keeping this commitment using legal loopholes. For example, in Israel, where by law 3 percent of employees in companies with over 100 employees must be people with disabilities, Google registers company employees as based abroad, thus making them officially "exempt."

13. For the most comprehensive benchmarking tools for disability inclusion, see About, Disability:IN, https://disabilityin.org/who-we-are/about/.
14. Paolo Gaudiano, "Google, Microsoft and Other Leaders Find Great Value in Employees with Disabilities," *Forbes*, November 6, 2017, https://www .forbes.com/sites/paologaudiano/2017/11/06/workforce-disability-conference /#20dedd8aa5e2.
15. In their 2020 D&I report, Google reports that 6 percent of its employees identify as having a disability, and it's entirely possible that the numbers were even bolstered by a few bright and capable employees with light attention deficit disorder (ADD) (in contrast, a full 20 percent of the world's population self-identify as having a disability). Nevertheless, Google's representation of people with disabilities in its workforce is dismally low—a third of what it should be. See *Google Diversity Annual Report 2020*, p. 21, https://kstatic.googleusercontent.com/files /25badfc6b6d1b33f3b87372ff7545d79261520d821e6ee9a82c4ab2de42a012 16be2156bc5a60ae3337ffe7176d90b8b2b3000891ac6e516a650ecebf0e3f866.
16. Cecile Daurat and Malcolm Scott, "Where Are America's Missing Workers?," *Bloomberg Newsletter*, October 14, 2021, https://www.bloomberg.com/news /newsletters/2021-10-14/what-s-happening-in-the-world-economy-the-search -for-america-s-missing-workers.

Chapter 2

1. Claire Cain Miller, Kevin Quealy, and Margo Sanger-Katz, "The Top Jobs Where Women Are Outnumbered by Men Named John," *New York Times*, April 24, 2018, https://www.nytimes.com/interactive/2018/04/24/upshot/women -and-men-named-john.html?auth=login-email.
2. IBM Policies, https://www.ibm.com/ibm/responsibility/policy4.shtml.
3. *Careers at Apple*, video, https://www.apple.com/careers.
4. Core Values, Coca-Cola Company, https://www.coca-colacompany.com /shared-future/people-values.
5. Equal Opportunity, Google Careers, https://careers.google.com/eeo/.
6. Testimony of Fatima Goss Graves, president and CEO National Women's Law Center House Committee on Education & Labor, Subcommittee on Civil Rights and Human Services and Subcommittee on Workforce Protections, Joint Subcommittee Hearing on the Paycheck Fairness Act (H.R. 7): Equal Pay for Equal Work, February 13, 2019, p. 4.
7. Kavya Vaghul, Sara Horowitz, and Amanda Keating, *Important in the Time of Coronavirus*, JUST Capital, 2019–2020, https://justcapital.com/reports/just-jobs -analysis-why-pay-equity-is-still-critically-important-in-the-time-of-coronavirus/.
8. Sara Harrison, "Five Years of Tech Diversity Reports—and Little Progress," *WIRED*, October 1, 2019, https://www.wired.com/story/five-years-tech-diversity -reports-little-progress/.
9. Dominic Abrams, Diane M. Houston, Julie Van de Vyver, and Milica Vasiljevic, "Equality Hypocrisy, Inconsistency, and Prejudice: The Unequal Application of

the Universal Human Right to Equality," *Peace and Conflict: Journal of Peace Psychology*, vol. 21, no. 1, February 2015, pp. 28–46, doi: 10.1037/pac0000084. This article was corrected after its publication. Correction in: *Peace and Conflict*, vol. 21, no. 3, August 2015, p. 358, PMCID: PMC4404755.

10. Seamus Roddy, *Diversity in the Workplace: New Data*, HR Clutch Report, May 14, 2020, https://clutch.co/hr/resources/diversity-in-workplace-statistics.

11. "The peoples of Europe, in creating an ever-closer union among them, are resolved to share a peaceful future based on common values. Conscious of its spiritual and moral heritage, the Union is founded on the indivisible, universal values of human dignity, freedom, equality and solidarity; it is based on the principles of democracy and the rule of law. It places the individual at the heart of its activities, by establishing the citizenship of the Union and by creating an area of freedom, security and justice." Charter of Fundamental Rights of the European Union, https://eur-lex.europa.eu/legal-content/EN/TXT/?uri=CELEX:12012P/TXT.

12. G. W. Harper, N. Jernewall, and M. C. Zea, (2004). "Giving Voice to Emerging Science and Theory for Lesbian, Gay, and Bisexual People of Color," *Cultural Diversity and Ethnic Minority Psychology*, vol. 10, no. 3, pp. 187–199, https://doi.org/10.1037/1099-9809.10.3.187.

13. Nicholas Eberstadt, *America's Invisible Felon Population: A Blind Spot in US National Statistics*, American Enterprise Institute, May 22, 2019, p. 4, https://www.jec.senate.gov/public/_cache/files/b23fea23-8e98-4bcd-aeed-edcc061a4bc0/testimony-eberstadt-final.pdf.

14. John Elflein, "Disability in the U.S.: Statistics and Facts," Statista, March 30, 2021, https://www.statista.com/topics/4380/disability-in-the-us/.

Chapter 3

1. Humphrey Taylor, chair, Harris Poll, *The Employment of Americans with Disabilities*, study conducted by Harris Interactive, conducted for Kessler Foundation and the National Organization on Disability (NOD), October 2010, https://smithct.org/assets/docs/Kessler-NOD-2010-Survey.pdf.

Chapter 4

1. Elizabeth Mendes and Lydia Saad, "For Unemployed, Length, Scale of Job Search Affects Well-Being," Gallup Wellbeing, blog, February 25, 2011, https://news.gallup.com/poll/146345/unemployed-length-scale-job-search-affects-wellbeing.aspx.

2. "Gender Pay Gap Statistics," Eurostat, https://ec.europa.eu/eurostat/statistics-explained/index.php?title=Gender_pay_gap_statistics.

3. Jacquelyn Smith, "7 Things You Probably Didn't Know About Your Job Search," *Forbes*, April 17, 2013, https://www.forbes.com/sites/jacquelynsmith/2013/04/17/7-things-you-probably-didnt-know-about-your-job-search/?sh=45f5738f3811.

4. World Health Organization, *World Report on Disability*, 2011, Table 8.2, p. 262, https://www.who.int/disabilities/world_report/2011/report.pdf.

5. It varies only due to different standards regarding what constitutes a disability (for instance, whether the data is based on "official" disability standards recognized by the Social Security Administration or based on self-reported data).

6. Dan Witters, "Caregiving Costs U.S. Economy $25.2 Billion in Lost Productivity," Gallop Wellbeing, blog, July 27, 2011, https://news.gallup.com/poll/148670/caregiving-costs-economy-billion-lost-productivity.aspx.

7. U.S. Department of Labor, Office of Disability Employment Policy, "Disability Employment Statistics," Labor Force Participation Rate, 2021, People with Disabilities, https://www.dol.gov/agencies/odep/research-evaluation/statistics.

8. Marc Mauer, "Addressing Racial Disparities in Incarceration," *Prison Journal*, supplement to vol. 91, no. 3, September 2011, pp. 87S, 88S, https://www.sentencingproject.org/wp-content/uploads/2016/01/Addressing-Racial-Disparities-in-Incarceration.pdf.

9. For a compilation of studies on racial disparities in criminal justice, see Radley Balko, "There's Overwhelming Evidence That the Criminal-Justice System Is Racist. Here's the Proof," *Washington Post*, September 18, 2018, https://perma.cc/BE8AVHE2.

10. Sentencing Project, *Report to the United Nations on Racial Disparities in the U.S. Criminal Justice System*, April 19, 2018, UN-Report-on-Racial-Disparities.pdf.

11. Supreet Kaur, Sendhil Mullainathan, Suanna Oh, and Frank Schilbach, "Do Financial Concerns Make Workers Less Productive?" (working paper 28338, National Bureau of Economic Research [NBER], January 2021), doi: 10.3386/w28338.

12. The solution to this paradox isn't of course to stop or cut disability pensions and benefits at all. Rather, we need to create workplace cultures and environments that facilitate and enhance the gradual transitions in self-identity from inability to ability. More about this in following chapters.

13. Mehmet C. Kocakulah, Ann Galligan Kelley, Krystal M. Mitchell, and Margaret P. Ruggieri, "Absenteeism Problems and Costs: Causes, Effects and Cures," *International Business & Economics Research Journal*, vol. 15, no. 3, May/June 2016, copyright by authors; CC-BY89 The Clute Institute.

14. Ibid.

15. *Health Inequalities in Europe*, EuroHealthNet, p. 3, https://eurohealthnet.eu/wp-content/uploads/documents/2019/191023_Factsheet_HealthEquityEU_WebLayout.pdf.

16. Barry Bosworth, "Increasing Disparities in Mortality by Socioeconomic Status," *Annual Review of Public Health*, vol. 39, April 2018, pp. 237–251, https://doi.org/10.1146/annurev-publhealth-040617-014615.

17. Carol S. North, Alina M. Suris, Rebecca P. Smith, and Richard V. King, "The Evolution of PTSD Criteria Across Editions of DSM," *Annals of Clinical Psychiatry*, vol. 28, no. 3, August 2016, https://pubmed.ncbi.nlm.nih.gov/27490836/.

18. M. Root, "Reconstructing the Impact of Trauma on Personality." In L. S. Brown and M. Ballou (eds.), *Personality and Psychopathology: Feminist Reappraisals* (New

York: Guilford, 1992), pp. 229–265; and L. S. Brown, "Not Outside the Range: One Feminist Perspective on Psychic Trauma." In C. Caruth (ed.), *Trauma: Explorations in Memory* (Baltimore: Johns Hopkins University Press, 1995), pp. 100–112.

19. Efi Ziv, "Trauma Ikeshet" ("Insidious Trauma"), Mafteach, 2012.
20. Kipling D. Williams and Blair Jarvis, "Cyberball: A Program for Use in Research on Interpersonal Ostracism and Acceptance," *Behavior Research Methods*, vol. 38, no. 1, 2006, pp. 174–180.
21. K. D. Williams and L. Zadro, "Ostracism: The Indiscriminate Early Detection System." In K. D. Williams, J. P. Forgas, and W. von Hippel (eds.), *The Social Outcast: Ostracism, Social Exclusion, Rejection, and Bullying* (New York: Psychology Press, 2005), pp. 19–34.
22. W. A. Warburton, K. D. Williams, and D. R. Cairns, "When Ostracism Leads to Aggression: The Moderating Effects of Control Deprivation," *Journal of Experimental Social Psychology*, vol. 42, no. 2, March 2006, pp. 213–220, https://doi.org/10.1016/j.jesp.2005.03.005.
23. N. I. Eisenberger, M. D. Lieberman, and K. D. Williams, "Does Rejection Hurt? An fMRI Study of Social Exclusion," *Science*, vol. 302, no. 5643, October 10, 2003, pp. 290–292.
24. See, for example, L. Smart Richman and M. R. Leary, "Reactions to Discrimination, Stigmatization, Ostracism, and Other Forms of Interpersonal Rejection: A Multimotive Model," *Psychological Review*, vol. 116, no. 2, 2009, p. 365.

Chapter 5

1. "Eight Surprising Facts About Hiring Employees," *Jamie VC*, https://jamievc.com/facts-about-hiring-employees/.
2. G. S. Shields, W. G. Moons, C. A. Tewell, and A. P. Yonelinas, "The Effect of Negative Affect on Cognition: Anxiety, Not Anger, Impairs Executive Function," *Emotion*, vol. 16, no. 6, 2016, pp. 792–797, https://doi.org/10.1037/emo0000151.
3. Grant S. Shields, Matthew A. Sazma, and Andrew P. Yonelinas, "The Effects of Acute Stress on Core Executive Functions: A Meta-Analysis and Comparison with Cortisol," *Neuroscience & Biobehavioral Reviews*, vol. 68, September 2016, pp. 651–668, ISSN 0149-7634, https://doi.org/10.1016/j.neubiorev.2016.06.038.
4. North Carolina State University, "Tech Sector Job Interviews Assess Anxiety, Not Software Skills," *ScienceDaily*, July 14, 2020, www.sciencedaily.com/releases/2020/07/200714101228.htm.
5. "Eight Surprising Facts About Hiring Employees," *Jamie VC*.
6. Frank Schmidt and John Hunter, "The Validity and Utility of Selection Methods in Personnel Psychology," *Psychological Bulletin*, vol. 124, no. 2, September 1998, pp. 262–274, doi: 10.1037/0033-2909.124.2.262.

Chapter 6

1. Jack Kelly, "More Than Half of US Workers Are Unhappy in Their Jobs: Here's Why and What Needs to Be Done Now," *Forbes*, October 25, 2019, https://www.forbes.com/sites/jackkelly/2019/10/25/more-than-half-of-us -workers-are-unhappy-in-their-jobs-heres-why-and-what-needs-to-be-done -now/?sh=1a5d3ee02024.

2. Christina Pavlou, "How to Reduce New Hire Turnover," *Workable*, https:// resources.workable.com/tutorial/new-hire-turnover-rate.

3. Reinhard Pekrun, Stephanie Lichtenfeld, Herbert W. Marsh, Kou Murayama, and Thomas Goetz, "Achievement Emotions and Academic Performance: Longitudinal Models of Reciprocal Effects," *Child Development*, vol. 88, no. 5, September-October 2017, pp. 1653–1670, first published February 8, 2017, doi: https:// doi.org/10.1111/cdev.12704.

4. National Institute of Mental Health (NIMH), "Social Anxiety Disorder: More Than Just Shyness," https://www.nimh.nih.gov/health/publications/social -anxiety-disorder-more-than-just-shyness.

Chapter 7

1. Clement Bellet, Jan-Emmanuel De Neve, and George Ward, "Does Employee Happiness Have an Impact on Productivity?" (working paper 2019-13, Saïd Business School, October 14, 2019), available at https://ssrn.com/abstract =3470734 or http://dx.doi.org/10.2139/ssrn.3470734.

2. C. H. DiMaria, C. Peroni, and F. Sarracino, "Happiness Matters: Productivity Gains from Subjective Well-Being," *Journal of Happiness Studies*, vol. 21, January 24, 2019, pp. 139–160, https://doi.org/10.1007/s10902-019-00074-1.

3. J. K. Harter, F. L. Schmidt, and C. L. M. Keyes, "Well-Being in the Workplace and Its Relationship to Business Outcomes: A Review of the Gallup Studies." In C. L. M. Keyes and J. Haidt (eds.), *Flourishing: Positive Psychology and the Life Well-Lived* (Washington, DC: American Psychological Association, 2003), pp. 205–224, https://doi.org/10.1037/10594-009.

4. Barry S. Hewlett, Hillary N. Fouts, Adam Boyette, and Bonnie L. Hewlett, "Social Learning Among Congo Basin Hunter-Gatherers," *Philosophical Transactions of the Royal Society B*, vol. 366, no. 1567, April 12, 2011, pp. 1168–1178, https://doi.org/10.1098/rstb.2010.0373.

5. Harter, Schmidt, and Keyes, "Well-Being in the Workplace."

6. Ibid.

7. Christian Krekel, George Ward, and Jan-Emmanuel De Neve, "Employee Well-being, Productivity, and Firm Performance" (working paper 2019-04, Saïd Business School, March 3, 2019), available at https://ssrn.com/abstract=3356581 or http://dx.doi.org/10.2139/ssrn.3356581.

8. "The Top Ten Most Common Company Values," Lucidity, https://getlucidity .com/strategy-resources/top-ten-most-common-company-values.

9. Nate Dvorak and Niraj Patel, "It's Time for a Core Values Audit," Gallup Workplace, blog, October 5, 2018, https://www.gallup.com/workplace/243434/time-core-values-audit.aspx.

10. "About Half of Workers Are Concerned About Discussing Mental Health Issues in the Workplace; a Third Worry About Consequences if They Seek Help," American Psychiatric Association, https://www.psychiatry.org/newsroom/news-releases/about-half-of-workers-are-concerned-about-discussing-mental-health-issues-in-the-workplace-a-third-worry-about-consequences-if-they-seek-help.

Chapter 8

1. Bryan Robinson, "New Study Says Workplace Bullying on Rise: What You Can Do During National Bullying Prevention Month," *Forbes*, October 11, 2019, https://www.forbes.com/sites/bryanrobinson/2019/10/11/new-study-says-workplace-bullying-on-rise-what-can-you-do-during-national-bullying-prevention-month/?sh=77c51f0c2a0d.

2. Ibid.

3. "Build a Culture Where Every Employee Can Use Their Voice," Gallup Workplace, blog, https://www.gallup.com/workplace/215939/diversity-inclusion.aspx.

4. D. Kipnis, "Does Power Corrupt?," *Journal of Personality and Social Psychology*, vol. 24, no. 1, 1972, pp. 33–41.

5. G. A. Van Kleef, C. Oveis, I. van der Lowe, A. Luokogan, J. Goetz, and D. Keltner, "Power, Distress and Compassion: Turning a Blind Eye to the Suffering of Others," *Psychological Science*, vol. 19, no. 12, 2008, pp. 1315–1322.

6. A. D. Galinsky, J. C. Magee, M. E. Inesi, and D. H. Gruenfeld, D. H., "Power and Perspectives Not Taken," *Psychological Science*, vol. 17, no. 12, 2006, pp. 1068–1074.

7. S. T. Fiske, "Controlling Other People: The Impact of Power on Stereotyping," *American Psychologist*, vol. 48, no. 6, 1993, pp. 621–628.

Chapter 9

1. Accenture Research, *Getting to Equal: The Disability Inclusion Advantage*, 2018, https://www.accenture.com/_acnmedia/PDF-89/Accenture-Disability-Inclusion-Research-Report.pdf.

2. Lincoln Quillian, Devah Pager, Ole Hexel, and Arnfinn H. Midtbøen, "Meta-analysis of Field Experiments Shows No Change in Racial Discrimination in Hiring Over Time," *PNAS*, vol. 114, no. 41, October 10, 2017, pp. 10870–10875, first published September 12, 2017, https://doi.org/10.1073/pnas.1706255114.

3. OECD, *All Hands In? Making Diversity Work for All*, September 2, 2020, https://www.oecd.org/social/all-hands-in-making-diversity-work-for-all-efb14583-en.htm.

4. Tom Hanks in *A League of Their Own*, Columbia Pictures, 1992.

5. Lemon Tree Hotels Limited (LTHL), About Us, https://www.lemontreehotels.com/about-us.aspx.

6. Rehadat Ausgleichsabgabe, "Statistics on the Employment of Severely Disabled People," https://www.rehadat-ausgleichsabgabe.de/hintergrund/statistik/.

7. Susan Corby, Laura William, and Sarah Richard, "Combatting Disability Discrimination: A Comparison of France and Great Britain," *European Journal of Industrial Relations*, vol. 25, no. 1, March 5, 2018, pp. 41–56, https://doi.org/10.1177/0959680118759169.

8. Thomas Barnay, Emmanuel Duguet, Christine Le Clainche, and Yann Videau, *An Evaluation of the 1987 French Disabled Workers Act: Better Paying Than Hiring*, HAL Open Science, January 2016, https://hal.archives-ouvertes.fr/hal-01260162/document.

9. Julian Cuppage, "The World and Disability: Quotas or No Quotas?," iGlobal Law, London, December 11, 2013, https://www.igloballaw.com/the-world-and-disability-quotas-or-no-quotas/.

Chapter 10

1. Claire Cain Miller, Kevin Quealy, and Margo Sanger-Katz, "The Top Jobs Where Women Are Outnumbered by Men Named John," *New York Times*, April 24, 2018, https://www.nytimes.com/interactive/2018/04/24/upshot/women-and-men-named-john.html?auth=login-email.

2. https://careers.microsoft.com/us/en/job/1123220/Accessibility-Support-Specialist.

3. U.S. Department of Labor, "Hazard Pay," https://www.dol.gov/general/topic/wages/hazardpay.

4. U.S. Department of Labor, Occupational Safety and Health Administration, Section 3, Definitions, https://www.osha.gov/laws-regs/oshact/section_3.

5. Mark Pendergrast, *For God, Country & Coca-Cola: The Definitive History of the Great American Soft Drink and the Company That Makes It*, 2nd ed., rev. and expanded ([Nachdr.] ed.) (New York: Basic Books, 2004), ISBN 978-0-465-05468-8. Also, "Top Ten Bad Beverage Ideas," *Time*, http://content.time.com/time/specials/packages/article/0,28804,1913612_1913610_1913608,00.html; and David Pryor, "Classic to Be Sold Along with Widely Resisted New Formula," *Los Angeles Times*, July 11, 1985, https://www.latimes.com/archives/la-xpm-1985-07-11-mn-8439-story.html, accessed March 2022.

6. Andrew Bigford, "Last Run: Sergio Zyman," *SKI Magazine*, retrieved June 14, 2006.

7. Community for Creative Non-Violence, "Washington DC's Community for Creative Non-Violence with a Shelter with a 1,350-Bed Capacity," theccnv.org, retrieved January 11, 2014.

8. Rachel Swarns, "U.S. Reports Drop in Homeless Population," *New York Times*, July 30, 2008, https://www.nytimes.com/2008/07/30/us/30homeless.html.

9. Cyleste C. Collins, Rong Bai, David Crampton, Robert Fischer, Rebecca D'Andrea, Kendra Dean, Nina Lalich, Tsui Chan, and Emily Cherney, "Implementing Housing First with Families and Young Adults: Challenges and Progress

Toward Self-Sufficiency," *Children and Youth Services Review, ScienceDirect*, vol. 96, January 2019, pp. 34–46, doi:10.1016/j.childyouth.2018.11.025.

10. Wikipedia, s.v. "MeToo movement," https://en.wikipedia.org/wiki/Me_Too _movement.

11. Wikipedia, s.v. "Black Lives Matter (BLM)," https://en.wikipedia.org/wiki /Black_Lives_Matter.

Index

About the Author

Gil Winch, PhD, is a social entrepreneur and the founder of CY (Call Yachol), a 100 percent underdog company composed primarily of people with severe disabilities.

Harnessing over 30 years of experience as a leading organizational consultant working for large companies, Dr. Winch developed a new managerial model that goes from screening to onboarding to managing those whom others often overlook.

CY is a proving ground and showcase for his hiring and workforce building model. He discusses this in his TED Talk, "How We Can Use the Hiring Process to Bring Out the Best in People."

As a keynote speaker, Dr. Winch has shared the stage with Bill Clinton and other influential leaders.

Dr. Winch is the recipient of numerous awards for social entrepreneurship. In 2011, he was chosen by Israel's leading economic newspaper, *The Marker*, as one of the 100 biggest influencers on the Israeli economy. He earned his doctorate in psychology from Tel Aviv University in Israel, where he lives with his wife and two Vizslas.

For more information, visit GilWinch.com.